SpringerBriefs in Well-Being
and Quality of Life Research

For further volumes:
http://www.springer.com/series/10150

Mark D. Holder

Happiness in Children

Measurement, Correlates and Enhancement
of Positive Subjective Well-Being

 Springer

Mark D. Holder
University of British Columbia
University Way 3333
Kelowna, BC V1V 1V7
Canada

ISSN 2211-7644   e-ISSN 2211-7652
ISBN 978-94-007-4413-4   e-ISBN 978-94-007-4414-1
DOI 10.1007/978-94-007-4414-1
Springer Dordrecht Heidelberg New York London

Library of Congress Control Number: 2012935231

Printed on acid-free paper

Springer is part of Springer Science+Business Media (www.springer.com)

Acknowledgments

I would like to express my gratitude to my students and colleagues whose work contributed to the development of this book. In particular, the work of Robert Callaway, Kate Ball, Andrea Klassen, Ashley Love, Zoë Sehn, and Judi Wallace. I would also like to express a special thanks to Ben Coleman who has contributed to my research program for the past six years. I want to thank Courtney Chrusch for reading an early draft of this book, and to Phoebe Scotland and Maxine Crawford who contributed to both the exposition and content of this book.

Contents

Abstract

Research in psychology, medicine, psychiatry, and neuroscience has usually focused on illness, dysfunction, and treatment. Emphasizing pathology has led to important advances in many fields including the development of effective tools to diagnose and treat physical and mental challenges. However, a newly re-emerging field called positive psychology recognizes that research should also consider the factors that contribute to human flourishing. Researchers in medicine and psychology frequently ask a common question: "What is wrong with you and how can we fix it?" Positive psychology is concerned with a very different question: "What is right with you and how can we promote it?" Over the past two decades there has been an increased focus on studies of positive well-being, including happiness. These studies typically use samples drawn from adult populations, and to a lesser extent, adolescent, and elderly populations. Until recently, the investigation of children was largely ignored by positive psychology researchers despite that most adults across many cultures and continents report that they desire a high level of happiness for their children. This book summarizes the limited research on positive well-being in children, with a particular focus on their happiness. It starts with a discussion of the constructs of positive psychology (i.e., well-being, happiness, and life satisfaction), and then outlines the research that shows the importance of studying well-being. Next, it examines how researchers measure happiness and what these measures tell us about whether children are happy and how their happiness differs from adults. Following this, a few current positive psychology theories are discussed with the aim of suggesting their promise in understanding children's well-being. Next, the importance of individual differences, including culture and temperament, is discussed. Because studies have only recently identified several of the factors associated with children's happiness, this book ends with a discussion of how we might enhance children's well-being and suggests directions for future research.

Introduction

Several research disciplines are linked to the medical model and have a strong focus on diagnosis and treatment. These disciplines, including psychology, psychiatry, medicine, and neuroscience, emphasize the identification of what is wrong with a person and then try to eliminate the problems or at least alleviate the negative symptoms. A relatively new approach, now commonly referred to as positive psychology, is concerned with understanding and promoting positive well-being with the goal of enhancing human flourishing. Positive psychology is the scientific inquiry of the characteristics, strengths, virtues, and behaviors that contribute to that which makes life worth living. Positive psychology acknowledges the importance of assessing and eliminating negative states; however, it recognizes that science should not be confined to only the study of these states.

Positive psychology is not intended to supplant other traditional fields. These other fields have made, and continue to make, valuable contributions to human well-being. Research based on the "diagnosis and treatment" tradition has successfully contributed to the development of interventions and strategies that reduce suffering associated with everything from depression to neuro-degenerative disorders. Positive psychology is properly viewed as a complement to this traditional approach.

Therefore, if traditional science, and predominantly psychology has often asked, "what is wrong with you and how do we fix it?" positive psychology is now asking, "what is *right* with you and how do we *promote* it?" The first part of the question (i.e., "what is right with you?") includes an individual's cognitive assessment of their overall satisfaction with their life, and their affective assessment of their overall level of happiness. However, positive psychology is not limited to the study of life satisfaction and happiness. There are many additional attributes that contribute to what is right with you and make life worth living (e.g., optimism, hope, creativity, physical health, spirituality, resilience, gratitude, kindness, and love).

Chapter 1
Understanding the Construct of Positive Well-Being and Happiness

Positive psychology has focused research attention on positive subjective well-being. Subjective well-being has been conceptualized as an overarching construct comprised of several dimensions (Diener 2006). Many researchers acknowledge that subjective well-being is multifaceted and encompasses individuals' evaluations of at least three components of their lives: (1) a cognitive appraisal of one's life, (2) low but appropriate levels of negative affect, (3) and an affective appraisal of one's positive emotions. The first component involves a cognitive evaluation of a person's past, present, and future prospects which can all contribute to a person's rating of his or her overall satisfaction with his or her life. The second component emphasizes that well-being is comprised of low, but appropriate levels of negative affect. In other words, positive psychologists are generally not preoccupied with the elimination of all negative affect, and they do not view this elimination as necessarily beneficial. Recognizing the value of negative emotions such as sadness, regret, guilt, and depression is important for positive psychologists. This value includes providing a source of feedback for our choices from which we can learn from. Negative affect also provides us with motivation to change ourselves, modify our environment, or relocate to a different environment. The third component involves the affective appraisal and is generally more present oriented. It includes how one feels about the emotional components surrounding his or her life including his or her current or momentary state of happiness and his or her overall general condition of happiness.

Not only is the umbrella term "subjective well-being" multidimensional, but the components of subjective well-being are considered multidimensional as well. For example, the third component, the affective appraisal of one's positive emotions, may include a number of positive emotions and states such as contentment, joy, pleasure, euphoria, elevation, and happiness. In turn, each of these positive emotions and states can be conceptualized as multidimensional. Happiness, which has received some of the most extensive recent empirical investigation, can be used as an example of this multidimensionality. Researchers currently recognize qualitatively

M. D. Holder, *Happiness in Children*, SpringerBriefs in Well-Being and Quality of Life Research, DOI: 10.1007/978-94-007-4414-1_1, © The Author(s) 2012

different types of happiness. For example, hedonia refers to the type of happiness associated with immediate gratification usually related to sensory pleasures, whereas eudaimonia refers to the type of happiness derived from delaying gratification in order to experience long-term benefits associated with living a virtuous life. When Aristotle proclaimed that *"Happiness* is the meaning and the purpose of life, the whole aim and end of human existence" (Cook 1993), he was referring to eudaimonia. Aristotle's perspective, demonstrated in this quote, underscores the prominent position that happiness has occupied in the minds of great thinkers.

Though there is some agreement that positive subjective well-being includes affective and cognitive appraisal factors, as well as appropriately low levels of negative affect, there is no widely accepted agreement on how these dimensions interact to form a general model of subjective well-being (Busseri et al. 2007). The literature on positive psychology does, however, include descriptions of different theoretical models of positive well-being. For example, one model conceptualizes positive subjective well-being as a higher order latent variable, and the components of well-being (i.e., life satisfaction, high levels of positive affect and low levels of negative affect) as indicator variables. Though research has provided evidence in support of this model (Vitterso and Nilsen 2002), it is probably misguided to characterize subjective well-being as only the shared variance of its dimensions (Busseri et al. 2007). Alternative models also recognize the three dimensions of positive subjective well-being but differ in two ways: (1) in whether they conceptualize the three dimensions as being independent dimensions and (2) whether well-being can be operationalized as a collective score of these three dimensions (Busseri et al. 2007). Future research goals in positive psychology should include objectives leading to increased understanding and consensus on how the dimensions of well-being combine and influence each other in order to contribute to well-being.

Importantly, theory and research recognize that positive and negative emotions are not the extreme endpoints of single dimensions. For instance, the construct of happiness is not simply one anchor of a dimension with the opposing end anchored by sadness or depression. Happiness and depression represent separable, albeit related, constructs that are somewhat orthogonal dimensions. Research supports the perspective that depression and happiness represent independent dimensions and includes work suggesting that the correlates and predictors of happiness and depression may be different. In a study of the relationships between happiness and the traits and facets of personality, Cheng and Furnham (2002) examined the relations between happiness and loneliness (a sub-component of depression). They reported the expected negative correlation between happiness and loneliness, but a second important finding was that these two constructs are conceptually distinct, and have unique predictors. Aspects of friendships, extraversion, and low levels of neuroticism were all significant predictors of happiness and loneliness. Psychoticism and a lack of self-confidence were significant predictors of loneliness but not happiness. Therefore, these findings are consistent with the perspective that both the experience of loneliness and the conceptualization of this construct are not totally encompassed by the absence of happiness.

However, the absence of happiness does not fully encompass the construct, nor the experience, of loneliness either. Studies that rely on biological assays point to a similar conclusion. In a study of elderly women, seven biomarkers indicated that positive and negative well-being are independent aspects of mental health (Ryff et al. 2006). These independent biomarkers included neuroendocrine assays (i.e., cortisol, DHEA-S, and norepinephrine) and cardiovascular measures (i.e., HDL cholesterol, total/HDL cholesterol, systolic blood pressure, and waist:hip ratio). These measures were either correlated with positive or negative well-being but not with both. Only two biomarkers (i.e., weight and haemoglobin) were correlated with both positive and negative well-being (though, of course, in opposite directions for each type of well-being) suggesting that positive and negative well-being are not best conceived as opposite endpoints on a bipolar continuum. In summary, happiness and depression may not be opposite ends on a single continuum, but rather orthogonal, albeit negatively correlated, dimensions.

Research on the measures of positive and negative well-being is consistent with this characterization. Positive and negative well-being measures, though consistently negatively correlated, do not indicate singularity. For example, in a typical study, the Oxford Happiness Inventory and the Beck Depression Inventory were negatively correlated at -0.52. Though significant, this is far from a perfect correlation of -1.00 suggesting that the measures assess distinct independent constructs (Cheng and Furnham 2003; Valiant 1993). For children, even different measures of happiness show significant, but only modest positive correlations ranging from 0.30 to 0.60 (Holder and Klassen 2010). Furthermore, the time frame with which the relations between positive and negative affect are studied is important too. At a specific single moment in time, happiness and depression are strongly negatively correlated. When these constructs are assessed over a longer time period, they show greater independence, with happiness appearing to be more stable over time than depression (Valiant 1993). Together these findings suggest that the literature on depression in children, though relevant to the understanding of subjective well-being in children, will not lead researchers to a complete understanding of children's happiness and life satisfaction. Additional studies are required that focus expressly on positive subjective wellness in order to garner a comprehensive and complete understanding of children's well-being.

Though substantial research suggests that positive and negative well-being are correlated but independent constructs, other researchers have adopted the perspective that happiness and depression are two anchors of the same dimension, and can be adequately assessed using just one bipolar measure (Joseph et al. 2004; Joseph and McCollam 1992). As an example, the short depression-happiness scale (SDHS) (Joseph et al. 2004) is comprised of six items, and conceptualizes happiness and depression as anchoring opposite ends of one continuum. The SDHS has displayed good convergent validity with other established measures of depression and happiness (Joseph et al. 2004).

Given the lack of agreement and the conflicting research findings, future studies are required to improve and clarify the constructs and assessment of happiness and depression. Such research would allow for greater consensus among researchers as to whether it is most appropriate to consider these constructs as orthogonal dimensions or as opposite poles of a singular bipolar dimension. Additionally, this research needs to be conducted independently for children. Research may eventually lead to the conclusion that happiness and depression are independent dimensions for adults, but this conceptualization may not necessarily be accurate for children.

References

Busseri, M. A., Sadava, S. W., & Decourville, N. (2007). A hybrid model for research on subjective well-being: examining common–and component specific-sources of variance in life satisfaction, positive affect, and negative affect. *Social Indicators Research, 83*, 414–445.

Cheng, H., & Furnham, A. (2002). Personality, peer relations, and self-confidence as predictors of happiness and loneliness. *Journal of Adolescence, 25*, 327–339.

Cheng, H., & Furnham, A. (2003). Personality, self-esteem, and demographic predictions of happiness and depression. *Personality and Individual Differences, 34*, 921–942.

Cook, J. (Ed.). (1993). *The Rubicon dictionary of positive, motivational, life-affirming, and inspirational quotations*. New York: New York Rubicon Press.

Diener, E. (2006). Guidelines for national indicators of subjective well-being and ill-being. *Journal of Happiness Studies, 7*, 397–404.

Holder, M. D., & Klassen, A. (2010). Temperament and happiness in children. *Journal of Happiness Studies, 11*, 419–439.

Joseph, S., & McCollam, P. (1992). A bipolar happiness and depression scale. *The Journal of Genetic Psychology, 154*(1), 127–129.

Joseph, S., Linley, P. A., Harwood, J., Lewis, C. A., & McCollam, P. (2004). Rapid assessment of well-being: the short depression-happiness scale (SDHS). *Psychology and Psychotherapy: Theory, Research, and Practice, 77*, 463–478.

Ryff, C. D., Love, G. D., Urry, H. L., Muller, D., Rosenkranz, M. A., Friedman, E. M., et al. (2006). Psychological well-being and ill-being: Do they have distinct or mirrored biological correlates? *Psychotherapy and Psychosomatics, 75*, 85–95.

Valiant, G. L. (1993). Life events, happiness, and depression: the half empty cup. *Personality and Individual Differences, 15*, 447–453.

Vitterso, J., & Nilsen, F. (2002). The conceptual and relational structure of subjective well-being neuroticism, and extraversion: once again, neuroticism is the important predictor of happiness. *Social Indicators Research, 57*, 89–118.

Chapter 2
Why Study Children's and Adult's Well-Being, Including Their Happiness?

Positive psychology includes the measurement and enhancement of positive well-being including happiness. Throughout human history, achieving happiness has been recognized by philosophers and intellectuals as a highly prized goal. A quote from Spinoza demonstrates this: "Everyone wants continuous and genuine happiness" (Spinoza 1677/1985). A high value assigned to happiness is currently reflected in many populations. For example, 9,000 college students were sampled from 47 nations and given a list of twenty values including wealth, love, and health (Kim-Prieto et al. 2005). The students identified happiness as the most important value with only 3% reporting that they did not value it at all.

The consensus that happiness is of high value and represents a worthwhile goal is reflected in the perspective held by most adults that we want our children to be happy. In a study of over 10,000 people from 48 countries on six continents, adults were asked about their desires for their children's emotions (Diener and Lucas 2004). This study reported that overall, most people desire high levels of happiness for their children and this desire is similar across genders (i.e., for sons and daughters). Additionally, the findings did not vary appreciably as a function of the wealth of the adult respondent. The desire for happiness in children was particularly high for adult women who themselves experience high levels of happiness and/or live in nations with high levels of happiness, and also for adults from individualistic compared to collectivistic nations. Furthermore, adults' desire for children's happiness proved higher than their desire for fearlessness or anger suppression.

While the construct of happiness occupies a privileged position among intellectuals, and is highly desired by people from across the globe, happiness has received limited attention from empirical researchers, including psychologists. While research in the realm of positive psychology has increased dramatically in the past decade, it is widely acknowledged that positive psychology has been largely understudied. This neglect is demonstrated by an examination of PsycINFO, which is a commonly used database for locating research articles in psychology. A current search of PsycINFO returns 136,668 journal articles if the key word "depression" is used, but only returns 7,494 articles if the key word

M. D. Holder, *Happiness in Children*, SpringerBriefs in Well-Being and Quality of Life Research, DOI: 10.1007/978-94-007-4414-1_2, © The Author(s) 2012

"happiness" is used. More articles (30,536) are found if the more global term "well-being" is used, but it is still just a fraction of the number of articles related to depression. In short, aspects of positive psychology have received relatively little attention compared to the study of negative affect. However, this long-standing neglect is showing signs of being addressed. From 1990 to 2000, the ratio of articles on depression compared to happiness was almost 27:1, but over the last 5 years this ratio has improved to 17:1.

The limited attention researchers have given to positive psychology is partic-ularly evident when it comes to research on the positive well-being of children. Despite the seemingly universal consensus that happiness in children is highly valued, research on the predictors of happiness in children and interventions to promote happiness in children is still relatively meager. Most empirical work on happiness has examined adults, and to a lesser extent examined adolescents and the elderly (Mahon and Yarcheski 2002). Furthermore, investigations of positive well-being that do incorporate children often study the children in terms of their impact on the parents' happiness and life satisfaction, or the impact of childhood experiences and memories on the happiness of the individual once the individual has reached adulthood (e.g., Amato 1994). For example, Adams (1995) found that adult women with a history of childhood sexual abuse experience positive affect less often, and self-report lower levels of well-being than women who do not share this history.

This relative neglect of research on the well-being and happiness of children is somewhat surprising. Given that children's happiness is so highly desired by adults from nations that are wealthier, happier, and more individualistic (e.g., the United State of America; Diener and Lucas 2004), one would hope that research on children's happiness would be plentiful. After all, these are the nations that conduct a substantial amount of the world's research. The relative scarcity of research on positive well-being, and the emphasis on negative well-being, is not limited to research on children. If we return to the database PsycInfo again, we can make an additional point if this time we do not specify a particular temporal window. There is a ratio of almost 18:1 using the keywords "depression" and "happiness", respectively. When the keyword "children" is also used, the ratio is a slightly more encouraging 15:1, although the total number of articles is of course substantially less. However, the trend for research on children's happiness is not so encouraging. Limiting the search to just the past 5 years (i.e., 2006–2011), the ratio is 15:1 using the key terms "depression" and "happiness" for all articles, but when the search is restricted with the filter "children", the ratio increases to almost 18:1. Furthermore, there are only 411 hits in this 5-year window for articles using the keywords "happiness" and "children". Nonetheless, there are several recent studies that have included children with the purpose of ascertaining the predictors of children's happiness, and investigations which seek to enhance children's well-being (e.g., Ben-Arieh 2006; Dwivedi and Harper 2004; Holder and Coleman 2008).

A stronger focus on research investigating happiness and life satisfaction in children is warranted because these variables have been empirically linked to a wide variety of advantages and benefits, at least in adults and adolescents. For example, adolescents aged 16–18 years who self-reported the highest levels of life satisfaction, also reported higher levels of success in academics (e.g., academic achievement and attitudes toward education), social (e.g., relationships with parents and peers), and intrapersonal (e.g., experiencing meaning in life and a healthier lifestyle) domains (Proctor et al. 2010). Research has demonstrated that positive subjective well-being, including happiness, is associated with a wide array of highly desirable outcomes in adults. These include improved health, enhanced creativity, increased facial recognition and attention, more productivity and success in one's career, better social relationships, higher levels of hope, and more resilience and post-traumatic growth. The benefits of these outcomes are further elaborated below.

Health: Positive states including happiness are associated with better actual and perceived health. In a review of the literature, Veenhoven (2008) suggests that happiness plays a role in the prevention of illness in healthy populations, and is also a strong predictor of physical health in normal populations. However, the results do not clearly show that subjective well-being plays an important curative role in those who are already ill (Pressman and Cohen 2005).

The relationships between well-being and health have been demonstrated in younger populations. For example, happiness was strongly positively correlated with the perceived health status, wellness, and clinical health of 12–14-year olds (Mahon et al. 2005). Though some theories suggest that this relationship is bidirectional (i.e., happiness is both a cause and result of good health; Argyle 1997), additional research is required to determine the causal direction of this relationship in younger populations (Van De Wetering et al. 2010). More studies that employ longitudinal designs would help shed light on this issue. Nonetheless, in a review of the research related to children's well-being and health, Dwyer et al. (2009) have pointed out the importance of encouraging children to participate in physical activity daily.

Optimism can be considered a facet of well-being and it is highly correlated with happiness. Like happiness, optimism is associated with improved health. The link between health and optimism has been assessed with physiological assays, showing that optimists possess a greater number of helper T cells, and increased natural killer cell cytoxicity which is related to better immunity (Barak 2006).

People with higher levels of subjective well-being are less likely to become ill and when they do become ill, they report less severe symptoms than people with lower levels of well-being. This relationship between susceptibility to illness and positive emotional style has been demonstrated in the excellent work of Cohen and his colleagues. For instance, in one experiment individuals were exposed to two different rhinoviruses (RV23 and RV39) to assess whether their emotional style was a factor in determining their susceptibility to developing the common cold (Cohen et al. 2003). Prior to exposure to the virus, the individuals' emotional style was assessed. Those who were identified as having a high positive emotional style (described in terms of positive adjectives such as happy, calm, or energetic) had a reduced chance of contracting a cold than those who were assessed as having a negative emotional style (described in terms of negative adjectives such as sad, tense, or hostile). In a companion study, individuals' susceptibility to a cold or the flu was assessed relative to their emotional style (Cohen et al. 2006). In this research, individuals were exposed to either Rhinovirus 39 (RV39) or Influenza A. Similar to the previous study, those who had a positive emotional style fared better. Following exposure to the rhinovirus or the influenza, those who initially were assessed with a more positive emotional style were less likely to contract an illness and reported less severe symptoms, if they did get sick. Interestingly, the health advantages associated with the positive emotional style were not strongly associated with engaging in more health-related strategies, or with an increase in the ability to cope with stress. The better health outcomes for those with a positive emotional style were largely a result of these individuals demonstrating a higher level of competence in their immune systems.

Understanding the influence of positive subjective well-being separately from negative well-being is critical because each factor may contribute independently to our health. Reviews of the literature have concluded that positive well-being may contribute to health and longevity above and beyond the contribution of negative well-being (Diener and Chan 2011). Cohen et al. (2003) reported that positive emotional style contributed to a reduction in one's susceptibility to illness and the severity of symptoms related to the common cold. However, they also discovered that negative emotional style contributed very little to participants' susceptibility to viral infection or symptom severity (although negative emotional style was associated with people identifying a greater number of unfounded symptoms, or symptoms that were not validated with objective markers of illness) (Cohen et al. 2003). In other words, positive well-being's capacity to improve health may be greater than negative well-being's capacity to undermine health. This understanding emphasizes and supports a fundamental perspective of positive psychology: it is crucial to understand and promote positive well-being and not restrict health practitioners' work to only addressing illness and dysfunction.

Given the improvements in immune functioning related to positive well-being, perhaps it is not surprising that individuals with higher positive well-being live longer as well. In an important recent review of the literature, Diener and Chan (2011) examined a wide range of research evidence including longitudinal studies, animal studies, experimental studies, and naturalistic studies. They concluded that high positive subjective well-being contributes 4–10 years of additional life compared to low subjective well-being. This is particularly striking given that these additional years tend to be experienced by happier people, and thus they are higher quality years characterized by greater happiness and better health. In one particularly interesting example of the relationship between positive well-being and longevity, researchers studied the journals of a sample of 180 Catholic nuns ranging in age between 18 and 32 years ($M = 22$) (Danner Snowden and Friesen 2001). They were able to evaluate the nuns' journals and rate the content in terms of the emotions they expressed (positive, negative, or neutral). These emotional ratings were then analyzed to determine whether the longevity of the nuns could be predicted based on the ratings. The researchers found that lifespan was longer for those nuns who described more positive emotions in their journals, compared to those nuns who described relatively few positive emotions. This difference in longevity was noteworthy; nuns whose journal ratings placed them in the top 25% of the nuns (i.e., they displayed the highest positive emotional content), lived almost 7 years longer than those nuns whose journal ratings placed them in the bottom 25% (i.e., those with the least positive emotional content). Longevity, particularly when it is accompanied by improved health and happiness, is a coveted goal most humans strive for. Given that positive emotional styles and well-being contribute to improved health and longevity, we may be able to encourage healthier children (and therefore also a healthier population over time) by enhancing their levels of happiness to promote longevity.

Enhanced Creativity: People who are happier tend to show higher levels of creativity, including the components of creativity. These components include the capacity to produce novel ideas, insights, and solutions that have practical applications to problems and challenges (Baas et al. 2008). Researchers understand the construct of creativity as being multifaceted; it is thought to be composed of several dimensions including cognitive flexibility (i.e., the range and number of categories one accesses while generating ideas as to the function of an object), fluency (i.e., the number of unique and new uses people can generate for an object presented to them), and originality (i.e., the degree to which the solutions generated are novel). It is possible that one can be creative in general, but be missing or have low levels of some of the dimensions of creativity (Baas et al. 2008). In such cases, creativity may be assessed by presenting a specific object (e.g., a brick) and challenging the individual to the task of generating as many novel and practical uses for the object as they can imagine. The individual may show high levels of overall creativity despite failing to generate uses beyond having the brick serve as an object contributing to building things (i.e., fail to recognize that a brick could be used as a weapon, or to displace water in the reservoir of a toilet to decrease water usage) thus showing low levels of cognitive flexibility (Baas et al. 2008).

In a meta-analysis of 102 studies reported over 25 years of research on emotions and creativity, Baas et al. (2008) concluded that positive moods lead to more creativity than neutral moods. The greatest impact of moods on creativity is when the moods are positive, activating, and linked to promoting positive states (e.g., happiness). Negative, deactivating moods, such as sadness, were not linked to creativity, and negative, activating moods associated with avoidance or escape (e.g., fear, anxiety) were related to decreased creativity. These relationships were reported across a variety of research designs (i.e., experimental and correlational) and samples were drawn from a range of populations (i.e., students and the general adult population). They were also observed when different dimensions of creativity were assessed (e.g., fluency, flexibility, originality, and eureka/insight).

Creativity, particularly as it relates to generating novel and practical solutions, is a desirable trait. Given that creativity is enhanced by positive states, including happiness, we may be able to enhance children's levels of creativity through happiness. Unfortunately, the experimental research exploring the causal relations between creativity and happiness in children is very limited. Future research is needed in order to ascertain whether happiness and creativity are associated in children and determine the causal directions of the relation between happiness and creativity.

Facial Recognition and Attention: The way people attend to certain objects or visual stimuli is highly influenced by the emotions and attitudes they are experiencing at that time. Research has consistently demonstrated that people are generally better at recognizing faces of people from their own race, than they are at recognizing faces of people from different races (Meissner and Brigham 2001; Slone et al. 2000). This bias, referred to as the Own-Race Bias, is robust and resistant to enduring change even with intensive hours of training (Lavrakas et al. 1976). The Own-Race Bias is found across a wide range of racial populations (Ng and Lindsay 1994; Teitelbaum and Geiselman 1997) but may be strongest for Caucasians when they perceive faces of racial minority populations (Meissner and Brigham 2001).

Johnson and Fredrickson (2005) investigated the impact of enhancing emotions prior to viewing faces (encoding), or after viewing the faces but prior to recognition. Participants viewed films selected to enhance joy or fear, or viewed films that were emotionally neutral. The researchers found that increasing joy either before or after viewing the faces significantly reduced the Own-Race Bias. They interpreted their results as supporting the Broaden and Build Theory (Fredrickson and Branigan 2005), claiming that positive affect serves to broaden the scope of attention, and thus facilitates global attentional processes. Additional studies support this theory by demonstrating that more positive emotional traits (e.g., happiness and optimism) enhance more global holistic processing. Negative emotional traits (e.g., anxiety) are associated with narrower local processing of elements which can be at the expense of more global or holistic processing (Basso et al. 1996). Thus negative emotions can lead to a situation that parallels the old adage that one cannot see the forest because of the trees.

Applying the Broaden and Build Theory to children suggests that children with greater positive subjective well-being should have cognitive advantages in the form of widened attentional scope. Empirical validation of strategies to reliably increase children's positive emotions could be used to help children become more open-minded and cognitively flexible.

Workplace and School Success: Success at work in the form of receiving a raise, an excellent job evaluation, a performance bonus, a promotion, or a job offer following an interview, certainly can improve happiness and life satisfaction, at least temporarily. However, recent research in positive psychology indicates that the relationship between our well-being and our success in the work place is bidirectional. Not only does success in the work place improve our well-being, but high levels of positive well-being can improve our career success. In other words, career success is often preceded by enhanced well-being.

Studies support the idea that positive well-being is an important contributor to career success (Georgellis et al. 2008; Martin 2005; Staw et al. 1994; Wright and Bonett 2007). One study concluded that workers who experience higher levels of happiness garner higher salaries and achieve better job performance than workers who have lower levels of happiness (Boehm and Lyubomirsky 2008). Given the previously discussed relationship between subjective well-being and health, it is not surprising that governments and corporations are interested in positive well-being in the workplace, as the mental health of their workers influences productivity. It is estimated that absenteeism and loss of productivity as a result of depression cost Canada $6.2 billion in 1998 and costs the United States between $44 and $51.5 billion annually (Lerner et al. 2004; Stephens and Joubert 2001). Having employees with higher well-being pays dividends. Employees who have higher levels of well-being generally experience less illness, miss fewer days of work, and display greater productivity and creativity in the workplace (Avey et al. 2006; Cohen et al. 1993; Hirt et al. 2008). As discussed above, the relationship between positive well-being and creativity may be particularly important in fields where creativity is essential. One can contrast this finding with data describing employees who are depressed. Though the average Canadian missed only 9.7 days of work in 2006, depressed Canadians missed over three times this number of days (Statistics Canada 2006; Statistics Canada 2007). The fact that these data were collected by a widespread governmental survey highlights the recognized importance of the consequences of affective status.

Although children may not be part of the work force, the relationship between positive well-being and the workplace for adults may be similar to the relationship between positive well-being and school for children. Conceivably, children who experience higher levels of positive well-being will miss fewer days of school and show increased productivity and creativity while at school. In fact, studies do show that hope, which is associated with life satisfaction and positive well-being (Gilman et al. 2006), is linked to increased academic success (Marques et al. 2009a). A 5-week intervention designed to increase hope in children 10–12 years of age increased life satisfaction, self-worth, and hope, but the trend toward an increase in academic achievement was not significant (Marques et al. 2011). It should be noted that academic achievement is particularly stable across time (Marques et al. 2009b), and thus may be somewhat resistant to change. To increase academic achievement, a lengthier intervention may be required.

Studies do show that personal attributes that are of interest to positive psychologists such as optimism and self-efficacy are associated with better academic performance. Research has reported that older students with higher expectations for success demonstrate greater achievement in mathematics (Meece 1996; Pintrich 2000; Pokay 1996). The link between self-efficacy and arithmetic skills has been demonstrated in younger children as well (Throndsen 2011). Increased self-efficacy may be responsible for increased academic success because children with higher self-efficacy try harder for longer periods (Schunk 1998) and select better strategies (i.e., more cognitive and metacognitive strategies) (Wolters and Pintrich 2001). Therefore, children's academic performance may benefit from positive psychology interventions that increase self-efficacy. This may be particularly important for children as they age; research indicates that compared to Grade 2, Grade 3 children demonstrate lower levels of optimism regarding their self-efficacy as it relates to basic skills in mathematics (Throndsen 2011).

Well-established theories related to positive psychology also suggest that positive well-being may contribute to the success of children in school. For example, Self-Determination Theory (SDT; Deci and Ryan 2000; Ryan and Deci 2000) claims that people in general and children in particular possess a natural motivation to learn and develop. According to this theory, learning is intrinsically motivated (i.e., learning is inherently interesting and enjoyable), and if the educational milieu in the home and classroom support this inherent inclination then children remain engaged and motivated in the learning process. SDT and supporting empirical research provide some guidelines for education that are in line with the perspectives of positive psychology. For example, meaningful choices can increase intrinsic motivation (Patall et al. 2008) whereas external rewards can undermine intrinsic motivation (Ryan and Deci 2009). The research suggests that both teachers and parents can promote children's well-being by supporting children's autonomy and intrinsic joy of learning, resulting in the children retaining more information, achieving higher grades, gaining greater perceived competence, and maintaining higher self-motivation (Ryan and Deci 2009).

Social Relationships: Social relationships are strongly associated with positive subjective well-being. In fact, some researchers contend that relationships are critical to our well-being (Diener and Seligman 2002; Lyubomirsky et al. 2005). Studies consistently report that individuals who score high in measures of subjective well-being also tend to enjoy more fulfilling social relationships (Lyubomirsky et al. 2005).

Given the pivotal role our social relationships play in contributing to our happiness, research investigating the links between children's happiness and their social interactions holds promise for improving children's well-being and understanding the impact of their relationships. Early work has shown that social relationships are related to children's happiness (Holder and Coleman 2009). For example, children who visit with friends more frequently are happier. Those who feel left out of social situations or agree that they cause trouble for their families are less happy.

Resilience and Post-traumatic Growth: The academic study of people thriving and experiencing low levels of negative affect did not suddenly begin with the introduction of the term "positive psychology". As early as 1955 a longitudinal study assessed the positive development of a large sample of children over several decades (Werner and Smith 1982, 1992). These children, during the first two years of their lives, faced naturally occurring adversities including growing up with poverty, family conflict, and parents with mental illness. Despite these serious challenges, one-third of these children who faced adversity developed into mentally and physically healthy and productive adults.

The phenomenon in which individuals develop successfully, and even thrive despite adversity, is known as resilience. A synthesis of 30 literature reviews on resilience concluded that children might be protected from the negative consequences of adversity depending on their prior experience and characteristics within three domains: individual (e.g., temperament), family (e.g., positive relationships with family members) and community (e.g., quality of the neighborhood they live in; Eriksson et al. 2010). Research also suggests that culture, gender, intelligence, the number of protective factors, and age at which one experiences setbacks all influence resilience.

More recently, research has linked resilience with positive well-being. Studies report that people who experience high positive well-being prior to facing adverse challenges have increased resilience to cope with and overcome difficult situations (Tugade and Frederickson 2007; Tugade and Frederickson 2004). For instance, the impact of negative and difficult challenges is mitigated by positive emotions (Tugade and Frederickson 2004). This mitigation may have important health benefits. People who self-report that they effectively cope with demanding negative challenges, more quickly return to their physiological baseline levels following a stressful event (Tugade and Frederickson 2004). Perhaps the negative physiological and psychological consequences of stressors can be buffered by improved subjective positive well-being via an increase in coping abilities (Tugade and Frederickson 2004).

Research investigating the factors that promote well-being may lead to interventions that increase our resiliency in the face of demanding negative challenges (Cohn et al. 2009; Tugade and Frederickson 2007). This could prove particularly important for those children who are faced with demanding and unfortunate situations ranging from experiencing the divorce of their parents to abuse.

Much of the research on the psychological impact of traumatic events has focused on the negative consequences of experiencing severely adverse events (e.g., post-traumatic stress disorder). However, research has shown that a significant number of people report that a traumatic event they experienced turned out later to be one of the best events that could have happened to them (Park 1998). This positive outcome, referred to as post-traumatic growth, is a fruitful line of current research. Post-traumatic growth is related to resilience in that they both involve positive responses to adversity. Post-traumatic growth is distinguished from resilience in that post-traumatic growth refers not just to maintaining current functioning following difficulties and trauma, but actually functioning at a higher healthier level following adversity.

The research on post-traumatic growth suggests that trauma may lead to improved psychological functioning despite, or even as a result of, the stress stemming from trauma (Calhoun and Tedeschi 2006; Joseph and Linley 2008). Growth following adversity has been studied and reported in war survivors (Lev-Wiesel and Amir 2006), parents having lost a child (Polatinsky and Esprey 2000), and women diagnosed with HIV (Updegraff et al. 2002). However, most of the research on post-traumatic growth is centered on adults, with less focus on adolescents and even less focus on children (Clay et al. 2009). Fortunately this lack of research on post-traumatic growth in children is starting to change with the development of psychometric instruments to assess children's post-traumatic growth (Cryder et al. 2006; see Kilmer 2006). However, it is of some concern that these instruments are generally modifications of existing instruments designed for adults. The domains of growth for children may not be exactly the same as those for adults and thus children may require different instruments to assess their growth.

Interim Summary and Conclusion: Positive well-being, including happiness, is associated with higher levels of creativity, better cognitive processing, broadening the scope of attention, improvements in immune functioning, increased longevity, and better physical and mental health outcomes. Greater productivity, success in the workplace, better social relationships, and stronger resilience are also stimulated by positive well-being (Avey et al. 2006; Cohn et al. 2009; Frey and Stutzer 2007; Hershberger 2005; Lyubomirsky et al. 2005; Mahon et al. 2005; Tugade and Frederickson 2004). People who experience higher levels of positive well-being also experience improved quality of sleep, have lower rates of suicide, and overall enjoy greater success in life (Koivumaa-Honkanen et al. 2001; Lyubomirsky et al. 2005). Some positive psychologists have taken the position that the capacities to be happy and satisfied with one's life are critical life skills in achieving successful adaptation and good mental health (Lyubomirsky et al. 2005).

The benefits associated with well-being, which have been empirically demonstrated primarily in the adult literature, potentially hold immense value for children. A broad-based meta-analysis of studies using a wide range of research approaches (e.g., correlational, longitudinal, and experimental) has led researchers to conclude that aspects of positive well-being are associated with many benefits (Lyubomirsky et al. 2005). Adults who enjoy high levels of positive well-being also enjoy several advantages in a wide range of important, valued domains of life (e.g., health, productivity, and social relationships) that are not shared by adults with low levels of well-being. This raises the possibility that children with high levels of well-being are likely to experience many of these advantages relative to children with low levels of well-being. In summary, research on well-being in children is important because it holds the promise of providing children with many of the benefits experienced by adults in a broad range of life domains. Additionally, the implications for lifelong functioning stemming from childhood well-being make research on childhood well-being a field with vast potential for improving human well-being. Although the research on adults' well-being may give us important insights into children's well-being, research on adults' well-being does not necessarily generalize to children's life satisfaction and happiness, as discussed in the next section.

Furthermore, knowledge derived from studies of negative well-being that focus on understanding the construct, measurement, predictors and strategies related to negative well-being may be of limited value in advancing our understanding of positive well-being. Current studies of well-being clearly open up the possibility that the components of positive well-being (e.g., happiness and life satisfaction) and the components of negative well-being (e.g., loneliness and depression) are not simply negatively correlated dimensions that lie on a single continuum, but represent more independent constructs. Therefore, positive well-being in general, and children's well-being in particular, need to be examined independently of depression and negative well-being.

Investigations of positive well-being in children, particularly happiness in children, are relatively sparse. However, research on children's well-being, including studies of children's happiness, is certainly feasible. Children aged 5–12 years possess the cognitive and affective maturity to allow for the study of their emotions in general and happiness in particular. During childhood, critical milestones of cognitive and emotional development are reached, including children's ability to recruit information from many sources to help understand and explain a wide range of their own emotions, and emotions of others (Berk 1994). For example, similar to adults, children can recognize that in a single environment one can experience many different emotions and can identify the causal factors that precipitated the emotions that they have experienced (Denham 1998; Whitesell and Harter 1989). Furthermore, even in a complex social milieu, children can recognize and label emotions (Schultz et al. 2004). As a result of this cognitive and emotional maturity, children can effectively participate in research and contribute insight into investigations of their emotions and their positive subjective well-being.

Research designed to uncover the predictors of subjective well-being in children, and to assess the efficacy of strategies designed to enhance children's well-being, is clearly warranted. For this research to be successful it is necessary to have valid and reliable measures of well-being. To illuminate the issues and challenges concerning the assessment of the different dimensions of well-being, the next section discusses the assessment of one of these dimensions: happiness.

References

Adams, C. L. (1995). The relationship of childhood sexual abuse to subjective well-being and depression for adult women. Dissertation Abstract International: Section B, The Sciences and Engineering, 56, 3430.

Amato, P. R. (1994). Father-child relations, mother-child relations, and offspring psychological well-being in early adulthood. Journal of Marriage and the Family, 56, 1031–1043.

Argyle, M. (1997). Is happiness a cause of health? Psychology and Health, 12, 769–781.

Avey, J. B., Patera, J. L., & West, B. J. (2006). The implications of positive psychological capital on employee absenteeism. Journal of Leadership and Organization Studies, 13(2), 42–60.

Baas, M., De Dreu, C. K. W., & Nijstad, B. A. (2008). A meta-analysis of 25 years of mood-creativity research: Hedonic tone, activation, or regulatory focus? Psychological Bulletin, 134(6), 779–806.

Barak, Y. (2006). The immune system and happiness. Autoimmunity Review, 5, 523–527.

Basso, M. R., Schefft, B. K., Ris, M. D., & Dember, W. N. (1996). Mood and global-local visual processing. Journal of the International Neuropsychological Society, 2, 249–255.

Ben-Arieh, A. (2006). Is the study of the State of our children changing? Re-visiting after 5 years. Children and Youth Services, 28, 799–811.

Berk, L. (1994). Child development (3rd ed.). Needham Heights: Allyn and Bacon.

Boehm, J. K., & Lyubomirsky, S. (2008). Does happiness promote career success? Journal of Career Assessment, 16(1), 101–116.

Calhoun, L. G., & Tedeschi, R. G. (2006). The handbook of posttraumatic growth: Research and practice. London: Lawrence Erlbaum.

Clay, R., Knibbs, J., & Joseph, S. (2009). Measurement of posttraumatic growth in young people: A review. Clinical Child Psychology and Psychiatry, 14, 411–422.

Cohen, S., Tyrrell, D. A., & Smith, A. P. (1993). Negative life events, perceived stress, negative affect, and susceptibility to the common cold. Journal of Personality and Social Psychology, 64(1), 131–140.

Cohen, S., Doyle, W. J., Turner, R. B., Alper, C. M., & Skoner, D. P. (2003). Emotional style and susceptibility to the common cold. *Psychosomatic Medicine, 65*, 652–657.

Cohen, S., Alper, C. M., Doyle, W. J., Treanor, J. J., & Turner, R. B. (2006). Positive emotional style predicts resistance to illness after experimental exposure to rhinovirus or influenza a virus. *Psychosomatic Medicine, 68*, 809–815.

Cohn, M. A., Fredrickson, B. L., Brown, S. L., Mikels, J. A., & Conway, A. M. (2009). Happiness unpacked: Positive emotions increase satisfaction by building resilience. *Emotion, 9*, 361–368.

Cryder, C. H., Kilmer, R. P., Tedeschi, R. G., & Calhoun, L. G. (2006). An exploratory study of posttraumatic growth in children following a natural disaster. *American Journal of Orthopsychiatry, 76*, 65–69.

Danner, D. D., Snowdon, D. A., & Friesen, W. V. (2001). Positive emotions in early life and longevity: Findings from the nun study. *Journal of Personality and Social Psychology, 80*, 804–813.

Denham, S. A. (1998). *Emotional development in young children*. New York: The Guilford Press.

Diener, E., & Chan, M. Y. (2011). Happy people live longer: Subjective well-being contributes to health and longevity. *Applied Psychology: Health and Well-Being, 3*, 1–43.

Diener, M. L., & Lucas, R. E. (2004). Adults' desires for children's emotions across 48 countries: Association with individual and national characteristics. *Journal of Cross-Cultural Psychology, 35*, 525–547.

Diener, E., & Seligman, M. E. (2002). Very happy people. *Psychological Science, 13*, 81–84.

Dwivedi, K., & Harper, P. (2004). *Promoting the emotional well-being of children and adolescents and preventing their mental ill health: A handbook*. London: Jessica KingsleyPublishers.

Dwyer, G., Bauer, L., Higgs, J., & Hardy, L. (2009). Promoting children's health and well-being: Broadening the therapy perspective. *Physical and Occupational Therapy in Pediatrics, 29*(1), 27–43.

Eriksson, I., Cater, A., Andershed, A., & Andershed, H. (2010). What we know and need to know about factors that protect youth from problems: A review of previous reviews. *Procedia Social and Behavioral Sciences, 5*, 477–482.

Fredrickson, B. L., & Branigan, C. (2005). Positive emotions broaden the scope of attention and thought-action repertoires. *Cognition and Emotions, 19*, 313–332.

Frey, B. S., & Stutzer, A. (2007). What can economists learn from happiness research? *Journal of Economic Literature, 40*, 402–435.

Georgellis, Y., Gregoriou, A., Healy, J., & Tgitgiauis, N. (2008). Unemployment and life satisfaction: A non-linear adaptation process. *International Journal of Manpower, 29*, 668–680.

Gilman, R., Dooley, J., & Florell, D. (2006). Relative levels of hope and their relationship with academic and psychological indicators among adolescents. *Journal of Social and Clinical Psychology, 25*, 166–178.

Hershberger, P. J. (2005). Prescribing happiness: Positive psychology and family medicine. *Family Medicine, 37*(9), 630–634.

Hirt, E. R., Devers, E. E., & McCrea, S. M. (2008). I want to be creative: Exploring the role of hedonic contingency theory in the positive mood-cognitive flexibility link. *Journal of Personality and Social Psychology, 94*(2), 214–230.

Holder, M. D., & Coleman, B. (2008). The contribution of temperament, popularity, and physical appearance to children's happiness. *Journal of Happiness Studies, 9*, 279–302.

Holder, M. D., & Coleman, B. (2009). The contribution of social relationships to children's happiness. *Journal of Happiness Studies, 10*, 329–349.

Johnson, K. J., & Fredrickson, B. L. (2005). "We all look the same to me"; positive emotions eliminate the own-race bias in face recognition. *Psychological Science, 16*, 875–881.

Joseph, S., & Linley, P. A. (Eds.). (2008). *Trauma recovery and growth: Positive psychological perspectives on posttraumatic stress*. Hoboken: Wiley.

Kilmer, R. P. (2006). Expert companions: Posttraumtic growth in clinical practices. In L. G. Calhoun & R. G. Tedeschi (Eds.), *The handbook of posttraumatic growth: Research and practice* (pp. 264–288). London: Lawrence Erlbaum.

Kim-Prieto, C., Diener, E., Tamir, M., Scollon, C., & Diener, M. (2005). Integrating the diversedefinitions of happiness: A time-sequential framework of subjective well-being. *Journal of Happiness Studies, 6*, 261–300.

Koivumaa-Honkanen, H., Honkanen, R., Viinamäki, H., Heikkila, K., Kaprio, J., & Koskenvuo, M. (2001). Life satisfaction and suicide: A 20 year follow-up study. *American Journal of Psychiatry, 158*, 433–439.

Lavrakas, P. J., Buri, J. R., & Mayzner, M. S. (1976). A perspective of the recognition of otherrace faces. *Perception and Psychophysics, 20*, 475–481.

Lerner, D., Adler, D. A., Chang, H., Lapitsky, L., Hood, M. Y., Perissinotto, C., et al. (2004). Unemployment, job retention, and productivity loss among employees with depression. *Psychiatric Services, 55*, 1371–1378.

Lev-Wiesel, R., & Amir, M. (2006). Resilience and posttraumatic growth in children. In L. G. Calhoun & R. G. Tedeschi (Eds.), *The handbook of posttraumatic growth: Research and practice* (pp. 248–263). London: Lawrence Erlbaum.

Lyubomirsky, S., King, L., & Diener, E. (2005). The benefits of frequent positive affect: Does happiness lead to success? *Psychological Bulletin, 131*, 803–855.

Mahon, N. E., & Yarcheski, A. (2002). Alternative theories of happiness in early adolescents. *Clinical Nursing Research, 11*, 306–323.

Mahon, N. E., Yarcheski, A., & Yarcheski, T. J. (2005). Happiness is related to gender and health in early adolescents. *Clinical Nursing Research, 14*, 175–190.

Marques, S.C., Lopez, S.J., & Pais-Ribeiro, J.L. (2009a). *Cross-sectional and longitudinal predictors of early adolescents' academic achievement.* Paper presented at the 11th European Congress of Psychology, Oslo, Norway.

Marques, S. C., Pais-Ribeiro, J. L., & Lopez, S. J. (2009b). *Cross-sectional and longitudinal predictors of early adolescents' academic achievement.* Paper presented at the 11th European Congress of Psychology, Oslo, Norway.

Marques, S. C., Lopez, S. J., & Pais-Ribeiro, J. L. (2011). "Building hope for the future": Strengths in middle-school students. *Journal of Happiness Studies, 12*, 139–152.

Martin, A. J. (2005). The role of positive psychology in enhancing satisfaction, motivation, and productivity in the workplace. *Journal of Organizational Behavior Management, 24*, 113–133.

Meece, J. L. (1996). Gender differences in mathematics achievement: The role of motivation. In M. Carr (Ed.), *Motivation in mathematics* (pp. 113–130). Creekskill: Hampton Press.

Meissner, C., & Brigham, J. (2001). Thirty years of investigating the own-race bias in memory for faces. *Psychology, Public Policy, and Law, 7*, 3–35.

Ng, W., & Lindsay, R. (1994). Cross-face recognition: Failure of the contact hypothesis. *Journal of Cross-Cultural Psychology, 25*, 217–232.

Park, C. L. (1998). Implications of posttraumatic growth for individuals. In R. G. Tedeschi, C. L. Park, & L. G. Calhoun (Eds.), *Posttraumatic growth: Positive changes in the aftermath of crisis* (pp. 153–178). Mahwah: Lawrence Erlbaum.

Patall, E. A., Cooper, H., & Robinson, J. C. (2008). The effects of choice on intrinsic motivation and related outcomes: A meta-analysis of research findings. *Psychological Bulletin, 134*, 270–300.

Pintrich, P. R. (2000). The role of goal orientation in self-regulated learning. In M. Boekaerts, P. R. Pintrich, & M. Zeidner (Eds.), *Handbook of self-regulation* (pp. 451–502). San Diego: Academic.

Pokay, P. A. (1996). Strategy use, motivation, and math achievement in high school students. In M. Carr (Ed.), *Motivation in mathematics* (pp. 157–172). Creekskill: Hampton Press.

Polatinsky, S., & Esprey, Y. (2000). An assessment of gender differences in the perception of benefit resulting from the loss of a child. *Journal of Traumatic Stress, 13*, 709–718.

Pressman, S. D., & Cohen, S. (2005). Does positive affect influence health? *Psychological Bulletin, 131*(6), 925–971.

Proctor, C., Linley, P. A., & Maltby, J. (2010). Very happy youths: Benefits of very high life satisfaction among adolescents. *Social Indicators Research, 98*, 519–532.

Ryan, R. M., & Deci, E. L. (2000). Self-determination theory and the facilitation of intrinsic motivation, social development, and well-being. *American Psychologist, 55*, 68–78.

Ryan, R. M., & Deci, E. L. (2009). Promoting self-determined school engagement: Motivation, learning, and well-being. In K. R. Wentzel & A. Wigfield (Eds.), *Handbook of motivation at school* (pp. 171–196). New York: Routledge.

Schultz, D., Izard, C. E., & Bear, G. G. (2004). Emotionality, emotion information processing, and aggression. *Development and Psychopathology, 16*, 371–387.

Schunk, D. H. (1998). Teaching elementary students to self-regulate practice of mathematical skills with modeling. In D. H. Schunk & B. J. Zimmerman (Eds.), *Self-regulated learning from teaching to self-reflective practice* (pp. 137–159). New York: The Guilford Press.

Slone, A., Brigham, J., & Meissner, C. (2000). Social and cognitive factors affecting the own-race bias in whites. *Basic and Applied Social Psychology, 22*, 71–84.

Spinoza, B. (1985). Ethics. In B. Spinoza (Ed.), *The collected writings of Spinoza* (Vol. 1, pp. 408–620). Princeton: Princeton University Press. Original work published in 1677.

Statistics Canada. (2006). *Work absence rates (Report No. 71-211-XIE)*. Retrieved from http://www.statcan.gc.ca/pub/71-211-x/71-211-x2007000-eng.pdf.

Statistics Canada. (2007). *Perspectives on labour and income- November 2007: Depression at work (Report No. 75-001-XWE)*. Retrieved from http://www.statcan.gc.ca/pub/75-001x/2007111/article/10406-eng.htm.

Staw, B. M., Sutton, R. I., & Pelled, L. H. (1994). Employee positive emotion and favourable outcomes at the workplace. *Organization Science, 5*(1), 51–71.

Stephens, T., & Joubert, N. (2001). The *Economic Burden of Mental Health Problems in Canada*. Retrieved from Public Health Agency of Canada: http://www.phac-aspc.gc.ca/publicat/cdic-mcc/22-1/d_e.html.

Teitelbaum, S., & Geiselman, R. E. (1997). Observer mood and cross-racial recognition of faces. *Journal of Cross-Cultural Psychology, 28*, 93–106.

Throndsen, I. (2011). Self-regulated learning of basic arithmetic skills: A longitudinal study. *British Journal of Educational Psychology, 81*, 558–578.

Tugade, M. M., & Frederickson, B. L. (2004). Resilient individuals use positive emotion to bounce back from negative emotional experiences. *Journal of Personality and Social Psychology, 86*, 320–333.

Tugade, M. M., & Frederickson, B. L. (2007). Regulation of positive emotions: Emotion regulation strategies that promote resilience. *Journal of Happiness Studies, 8*, 311–333.

Updegraff, J. A., Taylor, S. E., Kemeny, M. E., & Wyatt, G. E. (2002). Positive and negative effects of HIV infection in women with low socioeconomic resources. *Personality and Social Psychology Bulletin, 28*, 382–394.

Van De Wetering, E. J., Van Excel, N. J. A., & Brouwer, W. B. F. (2010). Piecing the jigsaw puzzle of adolescent happiness. *Journal of Economic Psychology, 31*, 923–935.

Veenhoven, R. (2008). Healthy happiness: Effects of happiness on physical health and the consequences for preventative health care. *Journal of Happiness Studies, 9*, 449–469.

Werner, E. E., & Smith, R. S. (1982). *Vulnerable but invincible: A study of resilient children*. New York: McGraw-Hill.

Werner, E. E., & Smith, R. S. (1992). *Overcoming the odds: High-risk children from birth to adulthood*. Ithaca: Cornell University Press.

Whitesell, N. R., & Harter, S. (1989). Children's reports of conflict between simultaneous opposite-valence emotions. *Child Development, 60*, 673–682.

Wolters, C. A., & Pintrich, P. R. (2001). Contextual differences in student motivation and self-regulated learning in mathematics, english and social studies classrooms. In H. J. Hartman (Ed.), *Metacognition in learning instruction: Theory, research and practice* (pp. 103–124). Dordrecht: Kluwer Academic Publishers.

Wright, T. A., & Bonett, D. G. (2007). Job satisfaction and psychological well-being as nonadditive predictors of workplace turnover. *Journal of Management, 33*(2), 141–160.

Chapter 3
The Assessment of Happiness in Adults and Children

Currently, positive psychologists have not reached a consensus on the single best practice to assess subjective well-being including happiness. As a result, researchers typically employ several measures. In a meta-analysis of 148 studies on the relationship between personality and well-being, DeNeve and Cooper (1998) found that the majority of studies (i.e., 91%) employed more than one measure of subjective well-being. However, the majority of these instruments were self-reports. Although this meta-analysis primarily focused on research that sampled from populations of adults, studies of children also tend to rely on multiple measures of well-being (e.g., Holder and Coleman 2008; Holder and Klassen 2010).

Given the lack of consensus as to the single most effective tool to assess well-being, several researchers have endorsed the common approach of employing multiple measures (e.g., Diener et al. 1991; Diener and Seligman 2004). This approach is sensible given that the constructs of positive subjective well-being, and even happiness, are likely composed of a number of facets. Thus, until a comprehensive multi-faceted measure is developed and tested, using multiple measures is considered appropriate to fully assess aspects of well-being, including children's happiness. Furthermore, there is no universally accepted definition of positive well-being or happiness so agreeing on a single ideal measure is difficult.

Self- and Other-Reports: Most research on well-being, including happiness, uses self-reports (Brunel et al. 2004; DeNeve and Cooper 1998; Lyubomirsky and Lepper 1999). The use of self-reports has been justified by noting that happiness is chiefly an individual and subjective phenomenon, and therefore, self-reports are appropriate and valid because each person is the critical judge of his or her own happiness (Lyubomirsky et al. 2005; Myers and Diener 1995). Furthermore, on a practical level, what is important to the individual and also important to clinicians, coaches, friends, and family, is how we perceive our own state of well-being.

Assessing happiness with self- or other report measures sometimes relies on questionnaires composed of a single item. Studies support the use of single-item

M. D. Holder, *Happiness in Children*, SpringerBriefs in Well-Being and Quality of Life Research, DOI: 10.1007/978-94-007-4414-1_3, © The Author(s) 2012

questionnaires showing them to be reliable and valid (Abdel-Khalek 2006; Harry 1976; Stull 1988; Swinyard et al. 2001). Measures comprised of a single item are most often employed to assess the enduring trait of happiness (see for example Andrews and Withey 1976; Cantril 1965). However, single item measures have been used to assess the current momentary state of happiness in participants as well (e.g., Fordyce 1988).

An example of a single item measure of happiness is the Faces Scale which has been adapted from early work by Andrews and Withey (1976). Typically, the Faces Scale is presented as a horizontal sequence of simple drawings of seven faces that are identical except that the mouths vary from very downturned (representing very unhappy) to very upturned (representing very happy). The ends of the line of faces are anchored with descriptor terms such as "most unhappy" and "most happy". We have frequently used this measure to assess happiness in children and found that it is easily understood by children 8–12 years of age including those with learning challenges (e.g., Holder and Coleman 2008). To estimate overall enduring happiness with the Faces Scale, we asked children to choose the drawing of the face that best represents how they usually feel (e.g., "Overall, how do you usually feel?").

Researchers of children's happiness include the Faces Scale as one or several estimates of children's happiness for several reasons. First, research has shown that children are better at recognizing and labeling emotions expressed in drawings of faces than when actual photographs are used (MacDonald and Kirkpatrick 1996), and the Faces Scales relies on drawings. Second, and more generally, in tests of comprehension for many different types of emotions, research has found that children are most skilled at labeling happiness and next most skilled at labeling sadness, the two emotions expressed on the Faces Scale (MacDonald and Kirkpatrick 1996). Third, research indicates that children prefer scales with more response options rather than fewer options (e.g., true/false options only) (Rebok et al. 2001). Therefore, the Faces Scale has an advantage for assessing children's happiness in that it employs seven response options (i.e., filling in one of seven circles corresponding to the seven drawings of faces). Fourth, the Faces Scale requires minimal instruction; researchers report that children almost immediately understand the scale and how to use it. Fifth, the Faces Scale requires only minimal language skills, so it can be used for a wide range of children including those with learning disabilities and perhaps even for those who are at a preverbal stage of develpment. Sixth, the Faces Scale can be used in group settings (e.g., in classrooms) as well as when children are tested individually. Finally, by changing the question associated with the Faces Scale from "Overall, how do you usually feel?" to "Right now, how do you feel at this moment?" we can use the same scale to assess momentary (i.e., state) happiness as well, thus expanding the uses of this scale and also enabling more direct comparisons between global and momentary happiness levels.

The Faces Scale is constructed like a visual analog scale (like a mercury thermometer) and research has shown that these scales are not understood by children as well as Likert-type scales, even when the children are given explicit instructions on how to use the visual analog scales (Shields et al. 2003). However, perhaps because of the simplicity and the straightforwardness of the scale, we have not had difficulty with children's comprehension of the Faces Scale.

As a supplement to single-item self-report measures of happiness like the Faces Scale, researchers have employed a variety of questionnaires that rely on multiple items (e.g., Hills and Argyle 1998, 2002; Kozma and Stones 1980; Lyubomirsky and Lepper 1999). Measures with multiple items now comprise the most widely used type of instrument to estimate happiness and life satisfaction (Lyubomirsky and Lepper 1999).

In general, questionnaires that utilize multiple items to estimate happiness in adults have been successfully used with children, with only minor modifications. For example, Lyubomirsky and Lepper (1999) developed a multi-item scale called the Subjective Happiness Scale, which demonstrates good reliability and validity. This scale is used to measure overall subjective happiness with four items (e.g., "Compared to most of my peers, I consider myself") which participants respond to on a 7-point Likert-type scale. However, the language complexity of this test exceeds the reading abilities of many children. Therefore, we adapted the test to better match the reading levels of children aged 8–12 years by simplifying the language where appropriate (Holder et al. 2010). In order to be confident that children as young as 8 years old could readily comprehend all the items of the scale, two items from the original scale were slightly simplified (Holder et al. 2010). The original wording of one question used in two items was, "To what extent does this characterization describe you?" We modified this question with the intent of simplifying it and used the following version for both items: "How much does this sentence describe you?" We have used this version to assess happiness in thousands of children and we have not experienced difficulties with its comprehensibility, even in children who do not have English as their first language. As an example, reliability ratings of this "child friendly" version of the Subjective Happiness Scale were acceptable with children aged 9–12 years in Canada (Holder and Klassen 2010), and 8–17 years in India (Holder et al. in press).

We have recently analyzed the Subjective Happiness Scale using Item Response Theory (Crawford et al. 2011). Item Response Theory is generally considered to be an improvement over Classical Test Theory as it assesses the reliability of each item of a test. Item Response Theory is used to determine how well each item of a test assesses the construct of interest and discriminates at different levels of the construct. Item Response Theory examines reliability of items across the full range of the construct of interest and identifies items that do not probe this construct. Our findings are consistent with the position that this scale does a good job of assessing the construct of happiness, particularly in differentiating people of low and medium levels of happiness. However, our analyses suggested that the scale may have two areas in which it can be improved. First, item number four lowered the reliability of the measure. Perhaps this is not surprising as the wording of this item might be confusing to some respondents. Respondents are asked to rate how much the following statement describes them:

"Some people are generally not very happy; though they are not depressed, they never seem as happy as they might be." A respondent might indicate that this statement does not at all apply to them either because they are very happy or they are very depressed. Second, the scale does not discriminate well for those who experience very high levels of happiness. Perhaps the scale could be improved by replacing the fourth item with one designed to distinguish between those with high levels of happiness. Measures of happiness in children, whether they are new measures or ones currently being used, would benefit from having Item Response Theory applied to them.

In addition to the Subjective Happiness Scale, researchers have assessed children's happiness with the Piers-Harris Children's Self-Concept Scale second edition (Piers Harris 2) (Piers and Herzberg 2002). The Piers Harris 2 is a standardized self-report questionnaire, with the short form comprised of 60 items and a response scale of "yes" or "no". The overall scale was developed to measure self-concept in 7–18-year-old children with a minimum of a grade two reading level. The Piers Harris 2 is reliable and valid (Marsh and Holmes 1990; Piers and Herzberg 2002) and assesses six dimensions of self-concept (Piers and Herzberg 2002). One of these domains, the happiness and satisfaction domain, uses 10 items with a true/false response option format to assess happiness and satisfaction in a child's life (e.g., "I am unhappy"). The Piers Harris 2 has the advantage, from a researcher's perspective, of being easily administered to small groups of individuals. The happiness and satisfaction domain of the Piers Harris 2 has been used in research as one indicator of children's happiness (Holder and Coleman 2008; Wood et al. 1996; Young and Bradley 1998).

The two measures discussed above are reliable and valid for use in children, and thus make appropriate research tools. However, multi-item self-report measures vary in their reliability and validity with respect to their assessment of happiness in children. For example, the Oxford Happiness Questionnaire, Short Form, created by Hills and Argyle (2002), is readily comprehended by children. Unfortunately, this questionnaire may be less reliable than other measures of children's happiness, as its reliability ratings in one sample of 9–12-year-old children were modest and lower than the reliability ratings of other measures of children's happiness (Holder and Klassen 2010). Given the lower reliability ratings, it is not surprising that this measure correlates rather weakly with some other measures of children's happiness. One reason for this is that the Oxford Happiness Questionnaire, which is comprised of 29 items instead of the eight in the short form, may be sensitive to more than just the respondent's happiness. Kashdan (2004) convincingly argues that the validity of the Oxford Happiness Questionnaire is suspect because it was not developed within a strong theoretical framework and did not have a clear definition of the construct being assessed. Furthermore, this questionnaire assesses numerous factors that are related to subjective positive well-being but not exclusive to happiness. These additional factors include self-esteem, sense of purpose and humor, social interest, kindness, and esthetic appreciation. As a result, the Oxford Happiness Questionnaire may be a useful tool for researchers to assess several dimensions of positive well-being, but its value in estimating only happiness in children is limited and conclusions from its use should reflect this limitation.

Researchers typically rely on multiple measures to accurately assess a construct, thereby giving them more confidence in their results. In general, each measure of a psychological construct typically has its own advantages, but they all rely on a certain set of assumptions. If the conclusions of a study are reached using an array of measures, and different measures usually rely on different assumptions, a researcher can be more assured that the conclusions reached do not depend on the unique assumptions of any one measure. This enables researchers to reach more confident conclusions that are more likely to meaningfully contribute to the literature.

Self-report measures, including those that assess happiness, all rely on the assumption that people have access to their "true" level of happiness and can accurately report this level. All individuals are not skilled at accessing this information, or are not honest in providing this information, so researchers often rely on additional measures, including other reports (e.g., estimates by spouses, or close friends) of the participants' well-being (Pavot and Diener 1993).

In the case of research on children, reports by knowledgeable others may include reports from parents and teachers. Relying on the reports of knowledgeable others (e.g., parents' ratings of their children) is accepted as a reliable and valid method of assessing personality (Funder 1991), as well as happiness and well-being (Lepper 1998). Specific to children, investigators have supported the use of multiple reporters (e.g., parents and children) when assessing temperament (Shiner and Caspi 2003). Temperament questionnaires completed by parents on behalf of their children are a valuable complement to children's self-reports because they may be less influenced by temporary moods and social desirability (Funder 1991). Parents are a particularly valuable source of assessing their children's psychological constructs. Although parents do not have direct access to their children's internal states, they have a rich awareness of their children based on many observations across different environments and times, making them one of the most accurate reporters of their children's functioning (Karp et al. 2004; Vaughn et al. 2002).

Research has found congruence between reports of children by parents and teachers, and the child's own report. For example, Holder and Coleman (2008) found that the self-report of children's own happiness was positively correlated with parents' and teachers' ratings of their child's happiness. However, these different estimates were only weakly, or at best moderately, correlated. Holder and Coleman found that parents' and teachers' ratings of children's happiness only correlated +0.15 even though they used a similar scale. It should be noted that research often finds that the correlations between ratings of children's psychological dimensions by parents and teachers are not strongly correlated (Achenbach et al. 1987; Gagnon et al. 1992). For example, the correlation of parents' and teachers' estimates of children's humor was only +0.14 and the correlation of their estimates of children's cheerfulness/optimism was only +0.14 as well (Martin et al. 2002). Unlike these low correlations, ratings by the same observer assessing the

same child across different situations are similar. For example, teachers' ratings of
the happiness of each child in two different situations (i.e., in class doing fun
activities and in class doing work) correlated at +0.57 (Holder and Coleman 2008).

Acceptable agreement has been found between children's ratings of their own
happiness (using the Faces Scale and the Subjective Happiness Scale) and parents'
ratings of their children's happiness (using the Faces Scale) with positive correlations ranging from 0.38 to 0.60 (Holder and Klassen 2010). Thus, the self- and
other reports of children's happiness demonstrate convergent validity. Similarly,
convergent validity is demonstrated in studies of adult happiness (Lyubomirsky
and Lepper 1999; Lyubomirsky et al. 2005; Myers and Diener 1995; Sandvik et al.
1993). For example, several different measures of adult happiness, such as peer
and spouse estimates of smiling behavior (e.g., Harker and Keltner 2001) and
physiological responses (e.g., Lerner, Taylor, Gonzalez, and Stayn as cited in
Lyubomirsky et al. 2005), all correlate positively. In general, research suggests
that there is an acceptable level of agreement between ratings made by self and by
knowledgeable others when children's happiness is being assessed, supporting the
perspective that self-reports are reliable and valid.

However, the general conclusion that self- and other reports show acceptable
agreement may have limited generalizability across cultures. In a recent study of
children's happiness based on samples of 440 children and their parents in
Northern India, we found relatively poor agreement between parents' ratings of
their children's happiness and children's self ratings when both reporters used
the Faces Scale (Holder et al. in press). These findings may indicate that culture-
specific assessment of research tools may be required or that additional methods must be employed when doing cross-cultural research on happiness in children. As an alternative to self- and other reports, researchers can assess subjective
well-being using personal interviews carried out by trained clinicians or investigators (Diener 1994). This approach is not typically used in research to assess
happiness in children, perhaps because of the required cost in terms of time and
money.

Experience Sample Method: An additional method, the Experience Sampling Method, has been employed by researchers to estimate happiness
(Csikszentmihalyi and Hunter 2003; Schimmack 2003). The Experience Sampling
Method typically uses some form of a pager (e.g., beeper, phone app, or pro-
grammable stopwatch) to signal participants at random times throughout each day
over a period of a week or two. When paged, the participants rate their current
levels of a dimension of well-being (e.g., happiness) as well as some additional
information (e.g., who they are with and what they are doing). Though individual
responses may primarily reflect momentary happiness, responses over a week or
two can be combined to give an estimate of a more enduring, trait-like level of
personal happiness. Using this technique, Csikszentmihalyi and Hunter (2003)
found that grade school children and youth were less happy when alone or when
engaged in school activities and most happy when they were with a friend. It is not
that keeping company with just any companion is linked to higher levels of
happiness; talking with parents is associated with just average levels of happiness.

Somewhat disappointing was the finding that those who spent more time reading for pleasure reported lower levels of happiness. Happiness levels not only varied with the activity the children were engaged in but also varied with the time of day; they were lower in the first few hours after waking up in the morning and during the hour just prior to going to bed. Of the days of the week, Saturday was associated with the highest levels of happiness whereas Monday was associated with the lowest levels.

Day Reconstruction Method: The Day Reconstruction Method is related to the Experience Sampling Method (Kahneman et al. 2004). In the Day Reconstruction Method participants are typically asked to systematically reconstruct from memory their previous day, reporting on their activities and experiences including their well-being. Procedures are put in place to mitigate recall biases as respondents attempt to recall their activities and feelings for each hour of that day. This research method is used infrequently to assess children's happiness, perhaps because the memory burden it places on participants may exceed what can reasonably be expected from children, particularly younger children.

The Experience Sampling Method is typically preferred by researchers over the Day Reconstruction Method due to the fact that the former is not as vulnerable to memory errors. However, the Experience Sampling Method places a substantial burden on the research participants in that it requires interruptions to their activities. A recent study of happiness and leisure directly compared the two approaches (i.e., the Day Reconstruction Method and the Experience Sampling Method) in adults and found that these measures of happiness gave a between-person correlation of 0.90 (Dockray et al. 2010). This suggests that both methods are reliable and valid.

Social Desirability: Given that happiness is a desired trait, at least in Europe and North America, studies that rely on self-report and other report estimates of happiness are potentially vulnerable to social desirable responding. Social desirable responding refers to the tendency of respondents, when completing self-report questionnaires, to respond in a manner that makes them appear in a favorable light by giving overly positive self-descriptions which may not be honest and/or accurate (Holtgraves 2004; Paulhus 2002).

Social desirable responding is a potential problem for research in many areas that rely on self-report measures including studies of attitudes, psychopathology, personality traits, and behaviors (Holtgraves 2004). For example, respondents often underreport the frequency they engage in behaviors that society typically disapproves of including drug use (Mensch and Kandel 1988), anal intercourse (Latkin et al. 1993), and hiring prostitutes (Brewer et al. 2000). Furthermore, people using self-report measures have been shown to underreport attitudes that are not socially condoned such as a dislike of condoms (Agnew and Loving 1998).

Social desirable responding is a particular concern for positive psychologists because research participants not only underreport behaviors and attitudes not favored by society, but they also *overreport* behaviors and attitudes that are favored by society. For instance, research that primarily relies on self-reports suggests that in the United States church attendance has remained stable at approximately 40%. However, a review of the literature indicated that when procedures are enacted to reduce social desirable responding, reporting of church attendance was reduced by about one-third (Presser and Stinson 1998). As well, respondents tend to overreport ethical behavior in the workplace (Randall and Fernandes 1991), the amount of physical exercise they engage in (Warnecke et al. 1997), and whether they hold politically correct attitudes including endorsing positive views toward women and negative attitudes toward patriarchal beliefs (Burris and Jackson 1999). A review of the literature suggests that social desirable responding can account for anywhere from 10 to 75% of the overall variance in responses to self-report measures, potentially undermining the validity of self-report measures (Nederhof 1985).

The concern that social desirable responding may undermine the validity of measures of positive subjective well-being is supported by the discrepancy between the typical findings of positive psychology and observations of human behavior in a variety of environments. For instance, Myers (2000) reported that 90% of people in the United States rate themselves as either "*pretty happy*" or "*very happy*." However, annually almost 10% of people in the United States experience depression (National Institute of Mental Health 2006). Additionally, the rate of divorce is approximately 50 and 40% in the United States (Myers 1992) and Canada (Statistics Canada 2005), respectively. These statistics seem at odds with research which typically reports that the majority of married couples commonly self-report that they are very happily married (Myers 1992). Using the faces scale we found that over 90% of children and adults self-report that they are in the top three most happy categories (Holder and Coleman 2008). Given this high level of self-reported happiness, it raises the possibility of social desirable responding in children.

Perhaps the apparent discrepancy between research findings and national statistics is attributable to social desirable responding. It is common for societies to emphasize that its members act in an agreeable and pleasant manner, even when an individual is experiencing a negative mood or an adverse situation (Eysenck 1990). According to Eysenck (1990), this emphasis promotes a compelling cultural expectation that negative affective states, including unhappiness, are not readily acceptable by society and should not be displayed around others. Thus, societal pressures may lead unhappy people to hide their negative states by imitating the actions of people who are genuinely happy, in order to be more accepted by society. Given these strong pressures, respondents may be biased when asked about their positive subjective well-being. As a result, self-reports of happiness may be artificially inflated because they are influenced by social desirable responding.

Social desirable responding has been studied for well over half a century (e.g., Edwards 1957; Meehl and Hathaway 1946). However, there have been very few studies that examine the impact of social desirable responding on the measurement of happiness and life satisfaction and not surprisingly, this void is magnified when it comes to studying happiness in children. It is of concern that the susceptibility of measures of subjective well-being to social desirable responding has not been fully assessed. Contamination of well-being measures by social desirability was investigated in two studies by Kozma and Stones (1987, 1988). They report that findings using self-report measures of well-being changed little whether or not social desirability was controlled. This suggested to the authors that the construct validity of several measures of well-being was not undermined by social desirability.

More recent work has investigated the influence of social desirable responding on one of the most widely used measures of positive subjective well-being, the Satisfaction with Life Scale. Diener et al. (1985) examined the relationship between the Satisfaction with Life Scale and the Marlowe Crowne Social Desirability Scale and concluded that social desirable responding did not unduly influence the former scale. In fact, the two scales were essentially not correlated ($r = 0.02$), suggesting that people who score high in social desirability respond similarly to those who score low in social desirability with respect to life satisfaction.

Research results do not always demonstrate that measures of social desirable responding and measures of positive well-being are unrelated. Unlike Diener et al. (1985), Carstensen and Cone (1983) reported that subjective well-being and social desirability were associated at least for their sample drawn from a population of elderly people. Furthermore, Diener et al. (1991) correlated several measures of positive subjective well-being with the Marlow Crowne Social Desirability Scale and found that social desirability is a strong predictor of happiness either when assessed with self-reports or other reports. The authors concluded that one can conceive of social desirability as a personality trait that actually promotes well-being and, therefore, should not be conceived as a contaminating factor.

However, studies designed to assess the susceptibility of measures of positive well-being to social desirability are limited in part because the conceptualization of social desirable responding used in these studies is incomplete. Most empirical research and theory are consistent with the perspective that socially desirable responding consists of at least two factors (Tan and Grace 2008). One factor involves self-deception in which a person has an inaccurately inflated self-view. This factor was originally called *self-deception* (Paulhus 1984) or *self-deceptive positivity* (Paulhus 1991), and now is referred to as *self-deceptive enhancement* (Paulhus 1991, 2002). This factor has been assessed with items from social desirability scales such as "I always know why I like things" and "I am fully in control of my own fate". Respondents may think that they are honestly responding to these items but their responses may be positively biased without their awareness. Therefore, these individuals are answering deceptively, but do not have an intention to do so. The second factor relates to when people knowingly deceive others by presenting an image of themselves that is inaccurate because it is overly positive. This factor is referred to as *impression management* (Paulhus 1984, 1991). Impression management is assessed with items from social desirability scales such as "I sometimes tell lies if I have to" and "I always obey laws, even if I'm unlikely to get caught". Individuals practicing impression management would deny and affirm these respective statements even though almost every person answering truthfully would give the opposite responses. A two-factor model of social desirable responding has received support from several research studies (Paulhus 2002).

When Diener et al. (1991) assessed the impact of Social Desirable Responding on the Satisfaction with Life Scale they only took into account the first factor, self-deceptive enhancement, in their conceptualization of social desirable responding. These researchers compared self-reported life satisfaction to reports made independently by interviewers. The reports completed by the interviewers would not be influenced directly by self-deceptive enhancement, but they might be biased by impression management. Thus, though both measures may be highly correlated, using other reports does not rule out the possible influence of social desirable responding. In fact, Diener et al. (1991) did recognize that some respondents may deliberately misrepresent themselves.

In a recent study not yet published, university students self-reported their well-being using several scales: the Faces Scale, Subjective Happiness Scale, Oxford Happiness Questionnaire-Short Form, and Satisfaction with Life Scale (Callaway and Holder, submitted). We used an experimental design that employed a two by three manipulation, with varied instructions that normally influence social desirable responding. One set of instructions was manipulated so that participants thought their responses would either be kept highly anonymous, or only somewhat confidential. The other set of instructions was manipulated so participants thought that either reporting high levels of happiness was common, or that reporting high levels of unhappiness was common (we also had a neutral set of instructions). Neither sets of instructions influenced the self-reports of subjective positive well-being. Furthermore, the measures of social desirability explained only 5–11% of the variance in the well-being measures. This is within the low range of other research that assesses the link between social desirable responding and psychological constructs other than well-being. These findings are consistent with the perspective that social desirability bias results only in minimal contamination for measures of happiness and life satisfaction.

Turning to new measures used in positive psychology, two relatively recent approaches have been employed to assess positive well-being: implicit measures and biological assays. Both of these approaches, if successful, could lead to reliable and valid measures of well-being that are not susceptible to socially desirable responding.

Implicit (disguised) Measures of Happiness: Implicit measures are disguised measures; participants are unaware of what is being assessed (Brunel et al. 2004). Implicit measures may prevent participants from presenting themselves in a more socially desirable (and less honest) way. A widely used implicit measure, the Implicit Association Test, presupposes that it is easier to pair a concept with attributes that have already been associated (Nosek et al. 2002; Swanson et al. 2001). For example, good (e.g., "love") and bad (e.g., "hatred") words were paired with either African American (black) or Caucasian (white) faces. Reaction times were lower for black faces paired with bad words and white faces paired with good words suggesting racial attitudes. Implicit measures helped validate a self-report measure of racial attitudes (Cunningham et al. 2001) and have been used to study self-enhancement, self-esteem, and life satisfaction (Jordan et al. 2003; Kim 2004; Kobayashi and Greenwald 2003).

There are only a few studies that assess implicit measures of well-being. The results of the one study (Kim 2004) were inconclusive because both the explicit and implicit measures of well-being had low retest correlations, and random measurement error was not well controlled. A second study found that the implicit and explicit measures were not well correlated, though self-report and other report measures were (Walker and Schimmack 2008). Overall, the goal of developing an implicit measure of positive subjective well-being that is not susceptible to social desirable responding remains unachieved. The authors suggested that implicit measures of positive well-being may have limited value for research in positive psychology. This may be the result of the nature of the constructs being assessed. In particular, life satisfaction involves the conscious awareness of one's evaluation of their life, and happiness involves the conscious awareness of one's emotions. If assessing the components of one's subjective well-being requires that one must first be consciously aware of their life satisfaction and happiness, then implicit measures may not accurately tap into these constructs.

Biological Assays: An alternative approach to assessing positive well-being, not susceptible to social desirable responding, utilizes biological assays. These assays could provide convergent validity for self- and other reports. There is already a well-established literature on the physiological correlates of negative well-being, including stress and depression. However, the complimentary literature on positive well-being is relatively meager. At this point in time, studies designed to identify the chemical, anatomical, and physiological correlates of positive subjective well-being have not fully matured, and overall the results do not clearly identify the biological markers of happiness or life satisfaction (Anderson and Tomenson 1994; Flory et al. 2004; Zald and Depue 2001). For example, in a recent report using adolescents, researchers found that cortisone levels, which correlate with negative emotions (e.g., self-reported stress, anxiety, and depression), were not correlated with self-reported happiness levels (Milam et al. 2011). In short, bio-logical assays have not been extensively used, have not been applied to assessing children's happiness, and fail to clearly identify a biochemical marker for hap-piness. Given that depression and happiness may not be opposite extremes of the same continuum as discussed earlier, then attempting to identify the biological markers for happiness by focusing on markers previously associated with depression may not be entirely successful. Perhaps fresh thinking and a new approach are required to select putative markers for happiness. There has been some success in identifying brain activity and well-being. In general, research indicates that increases in left prefrontal activity is associated with increased levels of well-being (Urry et al. 2004).

Interim Summary and Conclusions: In summary, researchers have developed several measures of the components of positive subjective well-being. These measures primarily rely on self-report and other report. There may be promise in developing implicit and biological measures of positive subjective well-being, though researchers have just recently begun this task. These measures have not yet been fully developed and have not been tested with children. Extensive future experimentation will be necessary.

By developing and using valid and reliable measures of the components of well-being, researchers have been able to identify the correlates and predictors of well-being. A review of these correlates and predictors is presented next.

References

Abdel-Khalek, A. M. (2006). Measuring happiness with a single-item scale. *Social Behavior and Personality, 34*, 139–150.

Achenbach, T. M., McConaughy, S. H., & Howell, C. T. (1987). Child/adolescent behavioral and emotional problems: Implications of cross-informant correlations for situational specificity. *Psychological Bulletin, 101*, 213–232.

Agnew, C. R., & Loving, T. J. (1998). The role of social desirability in self-reported condom use attitudes and intentions. *AIDS and Behavior, 2*, 229–239.

Anderson, I. M., & Tomenson, B. M. (1994). The efficacy of selective serotonin reuptake inhibitors in depression: A meta-analysis of studies against tricyclic antidepressants. *Journal of Psychopharmacology, 8*, 238–249.

Andrews, F. M., & Withey, S. B. (1976). *Social indicators of well-being.* New York: Plenum Press.

Brewer, D. D., Potterat, J. J., Garrett, S. B., Muth, S. Q., Roberts, J. M., Jr, Kasprzyk, D., et al. (2000). Prostitution and the sex discrepancy in reported number of sexual partners. *Proceedings of the National Academy of Sciences of the United States of America, 97*, 12385–12388.

Brunel, F. F., Tietje, B. C., & Greenwald, A. G. (2004). Is the implicit association test a valid and valuable measure of implicit consumer social cognition? *Journal of Consumer Psychology, 14*, 385–404.

Burris, C. T., & Jackson, L. M. (1999). Hate the sin/love the sinner, or love the hater? Intrinsic religion and responses to partner abuse. *Journal for the Scientific Study of Religion, 38*, 160–174.

Cantril, H. (1965). *The pattern of human concerns.* New Brunswick: University Press.

Carstensen, L. L., & Cone, J. D. (1983). Social desirability and the measurement of psychological well-being in elderly persons. *Journal of Gerontology, 38*, 713–715.

Crawford, M., Holder, M. D., & O'Connor, B. (2011). *Application of item response theory to measures of positive psychology.* Philadelphia: Second World Congress on Positive Psychology.

Csikszentmihalyi, M., & Hunter, J. (2003). Happiness in everyday life: The uses of experience sampling. *Journal of Happiness Studies, 4*, 185–199.

Cunningham, W. A., Preacher, K. J., & Banaji, M. R. (2001). Implicit attitude measures. *Psychological Science, 12*(2), 163–170.

DeNeve, K. M., & Cooper, H. (1998). The happy personality: A meta-analysis of 137 personality traits and subjective well-being. *Psychological Bulletin, 124*, 197–229.

Diener, E. (1994). Assessing subjective well-being: Progress and opportunities. *Social Indicators Research, 31*, 103–157.

Diener, E., & Seligman, M. E. P. (2004). Beyond money: Toward an economy of well-being. *Psychological Science in the Public Interest, 5*(1), 1–31.

Diener, E., Emmons, R. A., Larsen, R. J., & Griffin, S. (1985). The satisfaction with life scale. *Journal of Personality Assessment, 49*(1), 71–75.

Diener, E., Sandvik, E., Pavot, W., & Gallagher, D. (1991). Response artefacts in the measurement of subjective well-being. *Social Indicators Research, 24*, 35–56.

Dockray, S., Grank, N., Ston, A. A., Kahneman, D., Wardlu, J., & Steptoe, A. (2010). A comparison of affect ratingsobtained with ecological momentary assessment and the day reconstruction method. *Social Indicators Research, 99*, 269–283.

Edwards, A. L. (1957). *The social desirability variable in personality assessment and research.* New York: Dryden.

Eysenck, M. (1990). *Happiness: Facts and myths.* Hillsdale: Lawrence Erlbaum Associates.

Flory, J. D., Manuck, S. B., Matthews, K. A., & Muldoon, M. F. (2004). Serotonergic function in the central nervous system is associated with daily ratings of positive mood. *Psychiatry Research, 129*, 11–19.

Fordyce, M. W. (1988). A review of research on *the happiness measures;* a sixty second index of happiness and mental health. *Social Indicators Research, 20*, 355–381.

Funder, D. C. (1991). Global traits: A neo-allportian approach to personality. *Psychological Science, 2*, 31–39.

Gagnon, C., Vitaro, F., & Tremblay, R. E. (1992). Parent-teacher agreement on kindergartners' behavioral problems. *Journal of Child Psychology and Psychiatry, 33*, 1255–1261.

Harker, L., & Keltner, D. (2001). Expressions of positive emotions in women's college yearbook pictures and their relationship to personality and life outcomes across adulthood. *Journal of Personality and Social Psychology, 80*, 112–124.

Harry, J. (1976). Evolving sources of happiness for men over the life cycle: A structural analysis. *Journal of Marriage and the Family, 42*, 289–296.

Hills, P., & Argyle, M. (1998). Positive moods derived from leisure and their relationship to happiness and personality. *Personality and Individual Differences, 25*, 523–535.

Hills, P., & Argyle, M. (2002). The oxford happiness questionnaire: A compact scale for the measurement of psychological well-being. *Personality and Individual Differences, 33*, 1071–1082.

Holder, M. D., & Coleman, B. (2008). The contribution of temperament, popularity, and physical appearance to children's happiness. *Journal of Happiness Studies, 9*, 279–302.

Holder, M. D., & Klassen, A. (2010). Temperament and happiness in children. *Journal of Happiness Studies, 11*, 419–439.

Holder, M. D., Coleman, B., & Wallace, J. M. (2010). Spirituality, religiousness, and happiness in children aged 8–12 years. *Journal of Happiness Studies, 11*, 131–150.

Holder, M. D., Coleman, B., Singh, K. (in press). Temperament and happiness in children in India. *Journal of Happiness Studies.*

Holtgraves, T. (2004). Social desirability and self-reports: Testing models of socially desirable responding. *Personality and Social Psychology Bulletin, 30*, 161–172.

Jordan, C. H., Spencer, S. J., Zanna, M. P., Hoshino-Brown, E., & Correll, J. (2003). Secureand defensive high self-esteem. *Journal of Personality and Social Psychology, 85*(5), 969–978.

Kahneman, D., Krueger, A., Schkade, D., Schwarz, N., & Stone, A. (2004). A survey method for characterizing daily life experience: The day reconstruction method. *Science, 306*, 1776–1780.

Karp, J., Servin, L. A., Stack, D. M., & Schwartzman, A. E. (2004). An observational measure of children's behavioural style: Evidence supporting a multi-method approach to studying temperament. *Infant and Child Development, 13*, 135–158.

Kashdan, T. B. (2004). The assessment of subjective well-being (issues raised by the oxford happiness questionnaire). *Personality and Individual Differences, 36*, 1225–1232.

Kim, D. (2004). The implicit life satisfaction measure. *Asian Journal of Social Psychology, 7*, 236–262.

Kobayashi, C., & Greenwald, A. G. (2003). Implicit-explicit differences in self-enhancement for Americans and Japanese. *Journal of Cross-Cultural Psychology, 34*(5), 522–541.

Kozma, A., & Stones, M. J. (1980). The measurement of happiness: Development of thememorial university of newfoundland scale of happiness (MUNSH). *Journal of Gerontology, 35*, 906–912.

Kozma, A., & Stones, M. J. (1987). Social desirability in measures of subjective well-being: A systematic evaluation. *Journal of Gerontology, 42*(1), 56–59.

Kozma, A., & Stones, M. J. (1988). Social desirability in measures of subjective well-being: Age comparisons. *Social Indicators Research, 20*, 1–14.

Latkin, C. A., Vlahov, D., & Anthony, J. C. (1993). Socially desirable responding and self-reported HIV infection risk behaviors among intravenous drug users. *Addiction, 88*, 517–525.

Lepper, H. S. (1998). Use of other-reports to validate subjective well-being measures. *Social Indicators Research, 44*, 367–379.

Lyubomirsky, S., & Lepper, H. S. (1999). A measure of subjective happiness: Preliminary reliability and construct validation. *Social Indicators Research, 46*, 137–155.

Lyubomirsky, S., Sheldon, K. M., & Schkade, D. (2005). Pursuing happiness: The architecture of sustainable change. *Review of General Psychology, 9*, 111–131.

MacDonald, P. M., & Kirkpatrick, S. W. (1996). Schematic drawings of facial expression for emotion recognition and interpretation by preschool-aged children. *Genetic, Social, and General Psychology Monographs, 122*, 373–388.

Marsh, H. W., & Holmes, I. W. (1990). Multidimensional self-concepts: Construct validation of responses by children. *American Educational Research Journal, 27*, 89–117.

Martin, L. R., Friedman, H. S., Tucker, J. S., Tomlinson-Keasey, C., Criqui, M. H., & Schwartz, J. E. (2002). A life course perspective on childhood cheerfulness and its relation to mortality risk. *Personality and Social Psychology Bulletin, 28*, 1155–1165.

Meehl, P. E., & Hathaway, S. R. (1946). The K factor as a suppressor variable in the minnesota multiphasic personality inventory. *Journal of Applied Psychology, 30*, 525–564.

Mensch, B. S., & Kandel, D. B. (1988). Underreporting of substance use in a national longitudinal youth cohort: Individual and interviewer effects. *The Public Opinion Quarterly, 52*(1), 100–124.

Milam, J., Slaughter, R., & McConnell, R. (2011). Dispositional optimism and hair cortisol among adolescents. Paper presented at the 2nd world congress on positive psychology. Philadelphia, USA.

Myers, D. G. (1992). Love and marriage. In *The pursuit of happiness: Who is happy and why* (1st ed., pp. 155–176). New York: William Morrow & Company, Inc.

Myers, D. G. (2000). The funds, friends, and faith of happy people. *American Psychologist, 55*, 56–67.

Myers, D. G., & Diener, E. (1995). Who is happy? *Psychological Science, 6*, 10–19.

National Institute of Mental Health. (2006). Depression. Retrieved 20 Dec 2006, from http://www.nimh.nih.gov/publicat/depression.cfm#ptdep1.

Nederhof, A. J. (1985). Methods of coping with social desirability bias: A review. *European Journal of Social Psychology, 15*, 263–280.

Nosek, B. A., Banaji, M. R., & Greenwald, A. G. (2002). Math = me, me = female, therefore math ≠ me. *Journal of Personality and Social Psychology, 83*(1), 44–59.

Paulhus, D. L. (1984). Two-component models of socially desirable responding. *Journal of Personality and Social Psychology, 46*, 598–609.

Paulhus, D. L. (1991). Measurement and control of response bias. In J. P. Robinson & P. R. Shaver (Eds.), *Measures of personality and social psychological attitudes* (pp. 17–59). San Diego: Academic Press.

Paulhus, D. L. (2002). Socially desirable responding: The evolution of a construct. In H. Braun, D. N. Jackson, & D. E. Wiley (Eds.), *The role of constructs in psychological and educational measurement* (pp. 67–88). Hillsdale: Erlbaum.

Pavot, W., & Diener, E. (1993). Review of the satisfaction with life scale. *Psychological Assessment, 5*, 164–172.

Piers, E. V., & Herzberg, D. S. (2002). *Manual for the Piers-Harris children's self-concept scale* (2nd ed.). Los Angeles: Western Psychological Services.

Presser, S., & Stinson, L. (1998). Data collection mode and social desirability bias in self-reported religious attendance. *American Sociological Review, 6*(3), 137–145.

Randall, D., & Fernandes, M. E. (1991). The social desirability response bias in ethics research. *Journal of Business Ethics, 10*, 805–817.

Rebok, G., Riley, A., Forrest, C., Starfield, B., Green, B., Robertson, J., et al. (2001). Elementary school-aged children's reports of their health: A cognitive interviewing style. *Quality of Life Research, 10*, 59–70.

Sandvik, E., Diener, E. A., & Seidlitz, L. (1993). Subjective well-being: The convergence and stability of self-report and non-self-report measures. *Journal of Personality, 61*, 317–342.

Schimmack, U. (2003). Affect measurement in experience sampling research. *Journal of Happiness Studies, 4*, 79–106.

Shields, B. J., Cohen, D. M., Harbeck-Weber, C., Powers, J. D., & Smith, G. A. (2003). Pediatric pain measurement using a visual analogue scale: A comparison of two teaching methods. *Clinical Pediatrics, 42*, 227–234.

Shiner, R., & Caspi, A. (2003). Personality differences in childhood and adolescence: Measurement, development and consequences. *Journal of Child Psychology and Psychiatry, 44*, 2–32.

Statistics Canada. (2005). The Daily: Divorces. Retrieved 20 Dec 2006, from http://www.statcan.ca/Daily/English/050309/d050309b.htm.

Stull, D. E. (1988). A dyadic approach to predicting well-being later in life. *Research of Aging, 10*, 81–101.

Swanson, J. E., Rudman, L. A., & Greenwald, A. G. (2001). Using the implicit association test to investigate attitude-behaviour consistency for stigmatised behaviour. *Cognition and Emotion, 15*(2), 207–230.

Swinyard, W. R., Kau, A., & Phua, H. (2001). Happiness, materialism, and religious experience in the US and Singapore. *Journal of Happiness Studies, 2*, 13–32.

Tan, L., & Grace, R. C. (2008). Social desirability and sexual offenders: a review. *Sexual Abuse: A Journal of Research and Treatment, 20*(1), 61–87.

Urry, H. L., Nitschke, J. B., Dolski, I., Jackson, D. C., Dalton, K. M., Mueller, C. J., et al. (2004). Making a life worth living: Neural correlates of well-being. *Psychological Science, 15*, 367–372.

Vaughn, B. E., Taraldson, B. J., Cuchton, L., & Egeland, B. (2002). The assessment of infant temperament: A critique of the carey infant temperamant questionnaire. *Infant Behavior and Development, 25*, 98–112.

Walker, S. S., & Schimmack, U. (2008). Validity of a happiness implicit association test as a measure of subjective well-being. *Journal of Research in Personality, 42*, 490–497.

Warnecke, R. B., Johnson, T. P., Cha'vez, N., Sudman, S., O'Rourke, D. P., Lacey, L., et al. (1997). Improving question wording in surveys of culturally diverse populations. *Annals of Epidemiology, 7*, 334–342.

Wood, K. C., Becker, J. A., & Thompson, J. K. (1996). Body image dissatisfaction in preadolescent children. *Journal of Applied and Developmental Psychology, 17*, 85–100.

Young, R. M. R., & Bradley, M. T. (1998). Social withdrawal: Self-efficacy, happiness, and popularity in introverted and extroverted adolescents. *Canadian Journal of School Psychology, 14*, 21–35.

Zald, D. H., & Depue, R. A. (2001). Serotonergic functioning correlates with positive and negative affect in psychiatrically healthy males. *Personality and Individual Differences, 30*, 71–86.

Chapter 4
Predictors and Correlates of Well-Being

As discussed earlier, the number of studies of the correlates and predictors of well-being, as well as investigations of the effectiveness of interventions designed to enhance well-being, has started to grow impressively in the past 10 years, but most of these studies have been conducted with adults. Though this work is important, it may have limited generalizability to positive subjective well-being in children. This potentially limited external validity is evident in the fact that many of the factors empirically identified as being related to adults' well-being are not applicable to children. For example, research has linked being married (Efklides et al. 2003), satisfaction with one's job (Argyle 2001), the happiness level of one's spouse (Stull 1998), and having children (Efkildes et al. 2003) as all being associated with adults' well-being. These factors cannot generally account for variability in children's happiness because they are only typically experienced after childhood. This is particularly true of the influence of adult romantic relationships. A more detailed discussion of the role of romantic relationships in adults' well-being will help illuminate that a factor that is important to adults' happiness and life satisfaction is not necessarily important to children's.

Research indicates that our relationships, including those with our family members, close friends, and romantic partners, are of primary importance in our lives (Clark and Graham 2005). For young adults, romantic relationships are particularly critical (Arnett 2000) and most college students perceive that their romantic relationships are their most meaningful and closest relationships (Berscheid et al. 1989). A number of studies have found that being involved in a romantic relationship, along with the quality of that relationship, is associated with one's well-being throughout life (Campbell et al. 2005; Kamp Dush and Amato 2005; Keyes and Waterman 2003). The importance of the quality of a romantic relationship was underscored by Demir (2008) who reported that the quality of a romantic relationship explained 3–6% of the variance in young adults' happiness beyond the contribution of personality factors. In fact, for those young adults who are currently in a romantic relationship, the contribution of other non-romantic

M. D. Holder, *Happiness in Children*, SpringerBriefs in Well-Being and Quality of Life Research, DOI: 10.1007/978-94-007-4414-1_4, © The Author(s) 2012

friends to their well-being is significantly reduced (Demir 2010). In general, being involved in a romantic relationship characterized by high quality is an important predictor of positive subjective well-being (Myers 2000). For instance, people who are currently married tend to perceive themselves as happier compared to other people including those who are single (i.e., never married), divorced, or separated (Dush et al. 2008; Myers 2000; Proulx et al. 2007).

Not recognizing the importance of social relationships may undermine happiness. Adults who rated having a high income and job success as more important than having meaningful friendships and being married were twice as likely to self-report that they were unhappy (Myers 2000). The link between adults' happiness and marriage is found across cultures. For example, Stack and Eshleman (1998) reported that increased levels of happiness were associated with marriage in 16 of the 17 countries they assessed even after controlling for sociodemographic variables. The one exception was Northern Ireland. However, both satisfaction with household income and health were both more important predictors than marital status. Research has demonstrated that quality romantic relationships contribute to happiness over and above the influence of personality (Demir 2008) and married individuals report higher levels of happiness than those who are single (never married), divorced, separated (Dush et al. 2008; Myers 2000; Proulx et al. 2007) or cohabiting (Stack and Eshleman 1998).

Similar to romantic relationships, wisdom assessed with online self-report measures was positively correlated with adults' happiness, especially for people with low education (Bergsma and Ardelt (in press)). In fact, wisdom explained 9.2% of the variance in their happiness. However, because children's cognitive capacities are not as developed as adults, and wisdom peaks in one's fifties and sixties, wisdom is unlikely to play a major role in children's happiness.

Though research has identified many factors that are related to adults' happiness, these findings may have quite limited generalizability to children. The above discussion on romantic relationships and wisdom makes it obvious that many of the known predictors of adult happiness are simply not relevant in children, and unlikely to play an important role in children's happiness. These factors include wisdom, romantic relationships, job satisfaction, raising children, and the happiness level of one's spouse. As a result, additional factors such as personality traits and facets, also known to be associated with happiness, might explain a greater amount of the individual variance in children's happiness. Alternatively, or additionally, components that have not been associated with adults' happiness (e.g., satisfaction with the social and/or academic dimensions of grade school) might comprise an important area of study in understanding children's well-being.

Additionally, research investigating positive subjective well-being during different phases of the life span is crucial. For example, the predictors of life satisfaction, which is a critical dimension of positive well-being, can change from childhood to adolescence. Therefore, distinct subcategories of childhood may need to be assessed. Academic grades earned by children in Grade 2 but not those earned by youth in Grade 8, predict life satisfaction (Chang et al. 2003).

Furthermore, factors related to happiness appear to change throughout life, at least for adult men. To attain happiness, men look toward their family life during the period when they have children in grade school (Harry 1976). Before and after this period, men seek happiness outside of their families. Another clear example of how the predictors of happiness may differ as we age comes from investigations of religiousness. Research has shown that church attendance is positively correlated with higher levels of happiness for adults (Francis et al. 1998). However, church attendance is associated with lower levels of positive well-being in adolescents (Kelley and Miller 2007) and may be linked to slightly reduced levels of happiness in children as well (Holder et al. 2010). These examples serve as clear indicators that the specific point in lifespan development must be accounted for in happiness research and underscore the importance of developing a body of literature that elucidates factors related to childhood happiness. Without additional research with children, we cannot assume that the relations established between well-being and a wide range of factors for adults necessarily applies to children.

References

Argyle, M. (2001). *The psychology of happiness* (2nd ed.). East Sussex: Routledge.

Arnett, J. J. (2000). Emerging adulthood: a theory of development from the late teens through the twenties. *American Psychologist, 55*, 469–480.

Bergsma, A., & Ardelt, M. (in press). Self-reported wisdom and happiness: an empirical investigation. *Journal of Happiness Studies*.

Berscheid, E., Snyder, M., & Omoto, A. M. (1989). Issues in studying relationships: Conceptualization and measuring closeness. In C. Hendrick (Ed.), *Close relationships* (Vol. 10, pp. 63–91)., Review of personality and social psychology Newbury Park: Sage.

Campbell, L., Simpson, J. A., Boldry, J. G., & Kashy, D. (2005). Perceptions of conflict and support in romantic relationships: the role of attachment anxiety. *Journal of Personality and Social Psychology, 88*, 510–531.

Chang, L., McBride-Chang, C., Stewart, S. M., & Au, E. (2003). Life satisfaction, self concept, and family relations in Chinese adolescents and children. *International Journal of Behavioural Development, 27*, 182–189.

Clark, M. S., & Graham, S. M. (2005). Do relationship researchers neglect singles? Can we do better? *Psychol Inquiry, 16*, 131–136.

Demir, M. (2008). Sweetheart, you really make me happy: romantic relationship quality and personality as predictors of happiness among emerging adults. *Journal of Happiness Studies, 9*(2), 257–277.

Demir, M. (2010). Close relationships and happiness among emerging adults. *Journal of Happiness Studies, 11*, 293–313.

Dush, C. M. K., Taylor, M. G., & Kroeger, R. A. (2008). Marital happiness and psychological well-being across the life course. *Family Relations, 57*, 211–226.

Efklides, A., Kalaitzidou, M., & Chankin, G. (2003). Subjective quality of life in old age in Greece. *European Psychologist, 8*, 178–191.

Francis, L. J., Brown, L. B., Lester, D., & Philipchalk, R. (1998). Happiness as stable extraversion: a cross-cultural examination of the reliability and validity of the Oxford happiness inventory among students in the U.K., U.S.A., Australia, and Canada. *Personality and Individual Differences, 24*, 167–171.

Harry, J. (1976). Evolving sources of happiness for men over the life cycle: A structural analysis. *Journal of Marriage and the Family, 42*, 289–296.

Holder, M. D., Coleman, B., & Wallace, J. M. (2010). Spirituality, religiousness, and happiness in children aged 8–12 years. *Journal of Happiness Studies, 11*, 131–150.

Kamp Dush, C. M., & Amato, P. R. (2005). Consequences or relationship status and quality for subjective well-being. *Journal of Personality and Social Psychology, 22*, 607–627.

Kelley, B. S., & Miller, L. (2007). Life satisfaction and spirituality in adolescents. *Research in the Social Scientific Study of Religion, 18*, 233–262.

Keyes, C. L. M., & Waterman, M. B. (2003). Dimensions of well-being and mental health in adulthood. In M. H. Bornstein, L. Davidson, C. L. M. Keyes, & K. A. Moore (Eds.), *Positive development across the life course* (pp. 477–497). Mahwah: NJ Lawrence Erlbaum Associates.

Myers, D. G. (2000). The funds, friends, and faith of happy people. *American Psychologist, 55*, 56–67.

Proulx, C. M., Helms, H. M., & Buehler, C. (2007). Marital quality and personal well-being: a meta-analysis. *Journal of Marriage and Family, 69*, 576–593.

Stack, S., & Eshleman, J. R. (1998). Marital status and happiness: a 17-nation study. *Journal of Marriage and the Family, 60*, 527–536.

Stull, D. E. (1988). A dyadic approach to predicting well-being in later life. *Research of Aging, 10*, 81–101.

Chapter 5
Similarities and Differences: Correlations and Predictors of Positive Well-Being in Adults and Children

Researchers have investigated many of the possible correlates of subjective well-being including happiness. Their studies have identified a range of variables that are associated with well-being as well as variables not associated with well-being. Identifying these variables is important for at least two reasons. First, once identified, these variables can be examined using other research approaches, such as longitudinal methods, to go beyond a merely descriptive understanding of the variables linked to positive well-being. For example, given that social relationships are important to children's happiness (Holder and Coleman 2009), a group of children could be followed over several years to help determine whether the social relationships of children foster their greater happiness, and/or whether higher levels of happiness promote better and more social relationships. Second, the variables that are most closely linked to well-being should give researchers insight into developing interventions that may enhance children's well-being. An example of this is shown in research which suggests that of the dimensions of spirituality, children's relationships with others are particularly important to their happiness (Holder et al. 2010). Given this finding, researchers may want to examine strategies that nurture the communal domain of children's spirituality, and assess whether children engaging in these strategies demonstrate enhanced spirituality and happiness.

The following sections describe research on the correlates of children's well-being with a specific focus on those studies that investigate happiness. When appropriate and when specific research findings are available, these sections compare and contrast the research findings based on samples of children with those based on samples of adults.

Age, Gender, and Education of Children: Studies have identified many factors that share no relationship, or only a very weak relationship, with the well-being of adults and children. Research using adult participants has found that in general, several demographic variables (e.g., gender, education, and employment) are not

M. D. Holder, *Happiness in Children*, SpringerBriefs in Well-Being and Quality of Life Research, DOI: 10.1007/978-94-007-4414-1_5, © The Author(s) 2012

strongly linked to well-being including happiness (Amato 1994; Cheng and Furnham 2003; Ellison 1991; Lu and Lin 1998; Pinquart and Sorensen 2001).

Findings based on studies of children's happiness have generally reached the same basic conclusion that demographic variables are only weakly associated with happiness. For example, in terms of gender, most research reports that happiness levels are similar between boys and girls (e.g., Uusitalo-Malmivaara (in press)).

Research findings on the relationship between age and well-being have been somewhat mixed. Both longitudinal (e.g., Charles et al. 2001) and cross-sectional research (e.g., Mroczek and Alameida 2004) suggests that aging through adulthood is associated with a decrease in negative affect. In a longitudinal study that followed adults over 22 years, life satisfaction was found to initially increase with age until about age 65 at which time it then tends to decline (Mroczek and Spiro 2005). However, most of these studies do not inform us on subjective well-being in children, as they assess only older populations. For example, Mroczek and Spiro relied on a sample of 33–92-year olds with the large majority of these participants being between 40 and 85.

In a particularly well-designed investigation, both cross-sectional and longitudinal methodologies were incorporated to assess changes in both happiness and life satisfaction across a wide age range (Baird et al. 2010). This investigation found that positive well-being was relatively stable in middle adulthood but declined rather precipitously after 70 years of age. Though the authors discuss their results in terms of life satisfaction, their first study may be better thought of as assessing happiness (i.e., they asked participants, "how happy are you at present with your life as a whole?") whereas their second study assessed life satisfaction (i.e., they asked participants, "how dissatisfied or satisfied are you with your life overall?"). Additionally, the authors described their work as assessing changes in well-being over the lifespan, but did not include respondents below the age of 16 years. Therefore, though studies show that components of well-being do change with age, they typically do not include children. Given that happiness and life satisfaction show changes, albeit not dramatic changes with age, studies are still needed to assess children in order to truly enable conclusions "across the lifespan". Unfortunately, we cannot assume that the findings based on samples of adults generalize completely to populations of children.

Most studies in positive psychology do not account for the contribution of genetics to the variables of interest. Given that individual variation in demographic variables is at least partially attributable to genetics, Stones et al. (2011) have argued that the correlations reported between positive subjective well-being and demographic variables may be artificially inflated. Though Stones et al. (2011) base their conclusion mostly on the available adult literature, their argument should apply to the relationship between well-being and demographic variables in children as well. Therefore, the actual relationships between many demographic factors and well-being may be even weaker than the modest ones reported in the literature.

Given the widely recognized importance of the family environment on children, it is perhaps surprising that many aspects of the family have little association with children's positive well-being. For example, the happiness of children 9–12 years of age was not significantly correlated with the age of the children's mother or father, and only weakly correlated with the number of siblings that a child had (Holder and Coleman 2008). When another dimension of well-being, life satisfaction, was investigated, similar results were observed. Children's satisfaction with their own lives is not correlated with several demographic variables, including the child's age and gender, or the occupational status of the parents (Huebner 1991).

Perhaps most surprising is that studies of children's happiness (Holder and Coleman 2008) and children's life satisfaction (Huebner 1991) have failed to find a relationship between the marital status of the children's parents, and the children's positive well-being. Children are equally happy and satisfied with their lives whether their parents are married, separated, divorced, living together but not married, or living apart and not married. This result is consistent with findings from adolescent research showing that parental marital status was not associated with adolescent happiness (Cheng and Furnham 2003). Later in life, several variables involving family and friends, including whether one's parents divorce, do not contribute to adult happiness (Amato 1994; Argyle and Lu 1990). The conclusion that the marital status of a child's parents seems unrelated to the happiness and life satisfaction of that child is surprising given the extensive research suggesting that divorce has a negative impact on children. Research suggests that divorce is linked to lower levels of some aspects of well-being as self-reported by adolescents (Amato and Sobolewski 2001; see Grossman and Rowat 1995) as well as increased psychological distress (Rodgers et al. 1997).

The repeated finding that parental marital status is not strongly associated with children's happiness or life satisfaction is probably not because the parents' relationships are inconsequential to their children's well-being. Rather than the specific marital status being the important variable, it is likely that the quality of the relationship between the mother and father is critical. It is unfortunately easy to recognize the possibility and identify examples of parents, who even though remain married, do not experience healthy positive relationships with each other. When the parents' relationships are marked by frequent and/or intense conflict, the children may feel trapped and pulled between their parents and this difficult situation might undermine positive subjective well-being even if the parents do not divorce (Amato and Afifi 2006). Thus the quality of the relationships, both between the spouses and between each parent and the child, may be what is important. Family relationships are complicated, and the interactions among family members are likely to be important to children's well-being. For example, the effect of parental conflict seems to interact with divorce in impacting children's well-being (Amato 2006). Taken as a whole, the level of well-being experienced by a child may not be directly governed by the marital status of the parents, but rather by the quality, including closeness, of the child's relationships with their mother and father (Moxnes 2003). For instance, independently of the marital status of the parents, the positive well-being of adolescents tended to be higher if they experienced more involvement with their father (Flouri and Buchanan 2003).

Though parental marital status alone is not strongly associated with children's positive well-being, having children can influence their parents' happiness. The association between having children and the happiness of the parents depends on individual differences (Kohler 2005). For example, having children may decrease the happiness of single parents and parents who do not want children, but have no appreciable effect on the happiness of married parents. Furthermore, the first child tends to increase the mother's happiness but does not affect the father's happiness. Having additional children tends to lower the mother's happiness but again this has little effect on the father's happiness levels.

It seems that neither adults' nor children's well-being is strongly impacted by several demographic variables commonly thought to contribute to well-being and happiness. For the links between well-being and family-related variables, research indicates the relationships are not well summarized by broad generalizations. The relationships are nuanced and studies need to adopt a finer grain analysis including the consideration of many individual differences.

Leisure Activities: Current research often views leisure activities as positively contributing to overall well-being (Caldwell 2005). In fact, the contribution of leisure to subjective well-being may be greater than the well-established contribution of leisure to physical health (Sacker and Cable 2006).

Research in positive psychology has recognized three categories of leisure: (1) time marked by the absence of obligation, (2) activities that are freely chosen, and (3) activities that yield intrapersonal rewards (Csikszentmihalyi and LeFevre 1989). Historically there have been two competing views of the value associated with leisure. Ancient Greek philosophers, including Plato and Aristotle, thought that leisure was important to build character, experience pleasure, and develop virtue. The Protestant work ethic opposes the Greek tradition as it devalues leisure, viewing it as largely a waste of time. However, recent research has supported the contention that leisure is associated with important benefits.

Leisure (e.g., walking or gardening) provides several benefits to those who engage in it. Firstly, leisure can have a restorative function in that it can afford us the opportunity to recuperate from cognitive and/or physically demanding experiences. Secondly, leisure can have a cathartic component in allowing us to expend physical and/or emotional energy (e.g., tennis or dance). Thirdly, leisure can provide us with opportunities to learn and master new information and/or skills (e.g., reading or playing piano).

A fourth benefit of leisure may include promoting well-being. Some of the early research examining a wide range of leisure activities suggested that engaging in leisure and adopting a hobby was one of the principal means of positively influencing mood (Argyle 2001). A wide variety of leisure activities seem to promote well-being for a wide range of individuals. For example, modest increases in happiness were reported for adults from Britain after they took holidays (Gilbert and Abdullah 2004). Happiness ratings were higher in Chinese university students who participated in leisure activities (Lu and Hu 2005), and in Japanese elderly people who took up a hobby (Onishi et al. 2006) compared to those not participating in leisure pursuits.

Though many of the studies are correlational and therefore do not allow us to ascertain causality, a few studies suggest that engaging in leisure activities does increase, and stabilize, well-being. One study reported that the leisure activities of 15-year-old adolescents predicted the subjective well-being of these people years later when they were adults (Sacker and Cable 2006). In another study, students were assigned to groups that were instructed to engage in no activities, two activities, or twelve pleasant activities in a month (Reich and Zautra 1981). Students who engaged in two or twelve activities reported an increase in their quality of life. Additionally, life satisfaction in the elderly improved after leisure education, though this improvement was no longer apparent during an 18-week follow-up (Searle et al. 1998). It should also be noted, however, that not all the research findings indicate that participating in leisure is associated with improved positive well-being. Research on walking (Lu and Hu 2005), and reading for pleasure (Csikszentmihalyi and Hunter 2003), failed to report that these leisure activities were linked to increased happiness.

Many theories predict that participating in leisure activities should promote increases in subjective well-being for a variety of reasons. Engaging in leisure activities may serve as a buffer against the deleterious impact of negative experiences (Tedeschi and Calhoun 1995, 2004; Tedeschi et al. 1998). This position was supported and expanded by Caldwell (2005) who suggested that engaging in leisure may protect people from the effects of negative experiences by furnishing them with relaxation, distraction, social support, and feelings of competency and meaning. Although these theoretical positions have been developed primarily from research based on adults and adolescents, these positions may be relevant to children's well-being. For example, participating in leisure activities can promote social relationships in people, including children (Caldwell 2005), and social relationships are associated with children's happiness (Holder and Coleman 2008).

Often, people have a variety of leisure activities to choose from, and the choice of activity is voluntary (Lu and Hu 2005). In these cases, which activity a person selects is determined by individual interests and goals such as relaxation and excitement (Hills and Argyle 1998). When the choice of leisure activity is voluntary and based on individual interests, research suggests that leisure is associated with increased happiness, autonomy, and self-confidence (e.g., Csikszentmihalyi and Hunter 2003; Frederick-Recascino and Schuster-Smith 2003). The voluntary nature of the choice of leisure activity is deemed central to the contribution of leisure to well-being, according to the Self-Determination Theory (Deci and Ryan 1985a, b; Ryan and Deci 2000). By contrast, when the choice is not self-determined, but rather the choice is made by others, participating in leisure activities is related to decreased levels of self-esteem and increased levels of anxiety (Eccles et al. 2003; Frederick-Recascino and Schuster-Smith 2003; Vandell et al. 2005).

The issue of self versus other determination, in the relation between leisure and well-being, may be pivotal for children. Frequently, children's leisure activities are chosen by the children's parents, guardians, or teachers. As a result, children's well-being may not be associated with their leisure activities in the same manner as for adults.

An additional factor that may be important to the relationship between well-being and leisure is whether the leisure pursuit is active or passive. For adults, engaging in active leisure, including leisure related to sports, has been associated with increased well-being (Csikszentmihalyi and Hunter 2003; Hills and Argyle 1998). However, some studies suggest that engaging in passive leisure, such as reading alone, watching television, and using a computer, has been related to decreased well-being (Argyle 2001; Csikszentmihalyi and Hunter 2003; Shaw and Gant 2002). In a sample of adults with an average age of 46 years, Frey et al. (2007) found that watching television was associated with decreased overall life satisfaction. Those who were categorized as heavy television viewers reported feeling less safe, having less trust in others, experiencing more anxiety, and reporting that they participate in fewer social activities than people who watch less television. This is particularly concerning given the trend over the past several decades has been that the reduction in time spent working has been largely balanced against an increase in time spent watching television.

A recent study of happiness in children corroborated the findings based on investigations of adults. Holder et al. (2009) found that active leisure activities were positively correlated with happiness but that passive leisure activities were weakly negatively correlated with happiness. In a similar vein, one study concluded that physical activity, closely linked with active leisure pursuits, is positively correlated with psychological well-being in children (Parfitt and Eston 2005), while another study found that sedentary behavior is negatively correlated with well-being in adolescents (Ussher et al. 2007). These studies did not assess important dimensions of positive well-being, such as happiness, and instead primarily focused on negative well-being. Parfitt and Eston (2005) assessed anxiety and depression, and even their measure of self-worth/esteem included items that more accurately evaluated negative self-esteem. Similarly, Ussher et al. (2007) assessed well-being with the Strengths and Difficulties Questionnaire, which includes dimensions such as conduct problems and peer relationship problems. These studies focus on negative well-being and thus it is difficult to generalize their conclusions to positive well-being.

Research findings on the relationships between active and passive leisure and well-being are not always consistent. For example, recently Heo et al. (2011) found that Internet use (i.e., a passive form of leisure) can have personal benefits for some elderly persons. Those older adults who had an affinity for the Internet reported greater satisfaction with their leisure activities. This age group may use different aspects of the Internet and have different goals related to their Internet use than younger age groups. Additionally, or alternatively, older adults who use the Internet may be different from their peers in terms of personality (e.g., openness to new experience) and other variables which are associated with happiness. Another recent study recruited 666 adults aged 30–50 years from seven different countries (Vella-Brodrick and Freire 2011). When asked to list their hobbies and free time activities, the top four categories, in order, were: playing sports, intellectual pursuits, artistic activities, and using electronic media (e.g., television and the Internet). They did not find a relationship between satisfaction with life and whether the leisure activity was sedentary or active. Furthermore, they found that greater use of electronic media was associated with increased satisfaction with life.

Although it may seem reasonable to assume that physical activity promotes positive psychological well-being, and that sedentary activity promotes negative psychological well-being, the evidence from the adult literature is not consistent. Any conclusions regarding the relationships between children's well-being and leisure activities, both active and passive, should be viewed as tentative until additional studies are completed.

Personality and Temperament: Research concerning well-being has repeatedly demonstrated a strong association between adults' happiness and their personality traits. In an excellent meta-analysis, Steel et al. (2008) found that 39–63% of the variance in subjective well-being can be explained by personality. Specifically, the personality traits of extraversion and neuroticism are strongly linked to happiness. When the relationships between well-being, the Big Five personality factors and demographic variables, were examined, extraversion (positively correlated) and neuroticism (negatively correlated) were two of the strongest correlates of well-being (Gutiérrez et al. 2005). Finally, in a causal model of the relationship between personality and subjective well-being, it was proposed that personality, particularly the traits of extraversion and neuroticism, are more strongly associated with the affective component of well-being (e.g., happiness) than the cognitive (e.g., life satisfaction) component (Schimmack et al. 2002).

During infancy and childhood the components of personality are referred to as *temperament* because personality is thought to be still developing. In fact, stability in personality is not reached until early (Costa and McCrae 1994) or even mid adulthood (Shiner and Caspi 2003). Thus, childhood temperament is considered the attentional, activational, and affective core of personality.

Estimates of temperament usually rely on quantifying observable emotion but the emphasis is primarily on appraising negative emotions (Belsky et al. 1996). This emphasis can be attributed to at least three factors: (1) negative emotions are related to later problematic behavior, (2) negative emotions tend to be highly visible and gauged with less difficulty, and (3) parents are more responsive to negative emotions (Belsky et al. 1991). Despite the emphasis on negative emotions, Huebner and his colleagues have completed important work showing that components of temperament make an important contribution to positive aspects of well-being. For instance, they found that life satisfaction and dimensions of temperament are correlated in children aged 10–13 years of age (Huebner 1991). In particular, extraversion has a clear positive association with life-satisfaction and neuroticism is negatively correlated with life satisfaction (McKnight et al. 2002).

The Emotionality, Activity, and Sociability theory (EAS-theory) of temperament (Buss and Plomin 1984) has been used to understand the relationship between children's temperaments and their positive well-being. The EAS-theory proposes that a child's temperament is comprised of three traits: Emotionality, Activity, and

Sociability. Emotionality (chiefly negative) includes the inclination toward distress, and being readily and intensely upset. Sociability includes a greater preference for being with others than being alone. Activity includes a higher frequency, duration, and intensity of activities, and choosing high-energy activities over low-energy activities. Although it is not considered a trait, a fourth component of temperament recognized by the EAS-theory is Shyness. Shyness includes avoiding and escaping social situations and feelings of tension and distress.

Given that high levels of Sociability and low levels of Shyness parallel the adult trait of extraversion (Buss and Plomin 1984), it is not surprising that this combination is positively correlated with different measures of children's happiness (Holder and Klassen 2010). Gray (1991) proposed that extraversion is associated with positive affect because compared to introverts, extraverts feel more pleasure because they are "wired" for a heightened sensitivity to rewards and pleasures. Evidence that supports Gray's theory includes findings that extraverts respond more intensely to pleasurable stimuli (Larsen and Rusting 1997) and situations, including nonsocial situations (Lucas and Diener 2001). Likewise, it is not surprising that high levels of emotionality, the temperament trait which parallels the adult personality trait of neuroticism (Buss and Plomin 1984), are associated with low levels of happiness in children (Holder and Klassen 2010). Gray's theory postulates that neuroticism is rooted in biologically-based fear and anxiety responses. Research indicates that people high in neuroticism perceive stimuli and situations as more negative and adopt attributional styles that may undermine their well-being (Cheng and Furnham 2001). Both Gray's theory and the constructs of children's temperament are grounded in biology, and Gray's theory provides one explanation for why temperament is linked to children's well-being.

Taken together, the evidence suggests that children's temperament, like adult personality, is a predictor of well-being and happiness. In particular, individual temperament traits are related to children's happiness in the same direction as the personality traits of extraversion and neuroticism are related to adults' happiness.

Popularity: Research on the link between well-being and popularity in adults and children has yielded mixed results. On the one hand, Ostberg (2003) found increased levels of well-being in children as the child's status compared to his or her peers increased. On the other hand, Kasser and Ahuvia (2002) found that university students who placed a high value on popularity and personal image were less well adjusted in terms of the level and frequency of their happiness. However, it must be noted that highly valuing popularity is different from actually *being* popular, and therefore, the latter relationship does not discount the possibility that actual popularity contributes positively to well-being in adults. Furthermore, popularity and happiness correlate with similar variables. For example, both happiness and popularity are negatively correlated with thoughts of suicide in adolescents (Field et al. 2001), and acts of bullying in children (Slee 1993). Popularity, as estimated with the Piers Harris Self Concept Scale (second edition), is only weakly positively associated with multiple measures of happiness for children (Holder and Coleman 2008). Collectively, the data suggest that popularity contributes only modestly to children's happiness.

Physical Appearance: Research has investigated the relationship between appearance and well-being, because physical appearance is associated with many benefits that may enhance well-being. For example, based on 30 studies, a meta-analysis found that that people who are more physically attractive are viewed by others as being "more sociable, sexually warm, mentally healthy, intelligent, and socially skilled than unattractive people" (Feingold 1992). This bias in attributing positive characteristics to attractive people is found with children as well. For example, teachers rated children who were more attractive as more popular and intelligent even under experimental conditions in which the children's performance was held constant (Clifford and Walster 1973).

Some research has found a modest positive association between attractiveness and well-being. For example, happiness is higher in young adults who judge themselves as more attractive (Neto 2001). Similarly, happiness levels tend to increase in adult women as their self-ratings of sexual attractiveness increase (Stokes and Frederick-Recascino 2003). Though one study reported that happiness and well-being, assessed with multiple measures, are higher in people judged as more attractive (Umberson and Hughes 1987), subsequent research challenged these findings by claiming that attractiveness was not adequately assessed (Diener et al. 1995b). Using an improved research methodology, Diener et al. (1995a, b) reported that subjective well-being was only weakly correlated with attractiveness. In a study of fashion models who represent people who are particularly valued for their attractiveness, researchers found that the models actually had lower well-being than nonmodels (Meyer et al. 2007).

A study with children suggested that self-reports of attractiveness are not strongly associated with children's happiness. When the Piers Harris Self Concept Scale (second edition) was used to assess physical appearance, multiple measures of happiness were positively, but only weakly, associated with children's self-ratings of appearance (Holder and Coleman 2008).

Despite the conclusion that attractiveness may be only weakly linked to well-being, attractiveness may contribute to happiness indirectly. Based on the bias that leads people to assign more favorable properties to attractive people (Feingold 1992), there are very likely more opportunities for attractive people to engage in behaviors known to contribute to happiness, such as fostering strong social networks, than for their less attractive peers. These opportunities may translate into real advantages. People tend to attribute more positive characteristics to those adults who are judged as more attractive. This tendency may generalize to attractive children as well as the previously discussed research by Clifford and Walster (1973) suggests. Thus, to date, it appears that physical appearance is positively correlated with happiness in children, but this association is weak.

Social Relationships: Social relationships, including the quality of one's relationships with family members and friends, are some of the most critical contributors to adults' well-being (e.g., Demir and Weitekamp 2006; see Lyubomirsky et al. 2005). Furthermore, many activities that promote well-being involve social components. For instance, activities that have been empirically linked to increased well-being involve substantial social interactions and foster stronger social relationships: participating on sports teams (Hills and Argyle 1998), affiliating with like-minded others and receiving social support while being involved in religious or volunteer activities (Arygle 2001; Cohen 2002; Francis et al. 1998), and engaging in acts of kindness toward others (Otake et al. 2006). Perhaps the increase in well-being that accompanies these activities is attributable to the social component of these activities.

Not surprisingly, a positive association between happiness and social relationships has been reported for children as well (Holder and Coleman 2008). For instance, 9–12-year-old children who visited frequently with friends were happier than their peers who did not visit frequently with friends. Similar to their role in adults' happiness, social relationships are likely considered a critical component of children's happiness.

Dissimilarities between Adults and Children: When children were asked to report their theories of happiness, some of the factors they identified as contributing to their happiness were the same but others differed from those reported by older people. For example, 8–9-year-old children reported that hobbies, pets, and parents contributed to their happiness whereas 12–13-year olds reported material objects, people and pets, and 17–18-year olds reported people, pets, and achievements (Chaplin 2009). Though people across a wide age range agree that their social relationships are important to their happiness (Chaplin 2009; Crossley and Landridge 2005), preadolescent children identify additional factors that adolescents do not.

Research corroborates the lay theories of happiness reported by people of different ages. As discussed above, many factors that correlate and predict well-being in adults are similarly related to well-being in children. The factors that weakly, or fail to, correlate and predict well-being in adults (e.g., demographics) are also not strong predictors of well-being in children. Research also shows that there are some noteworthy differences between children and adults in the factors that correlate with well-being, and there are even differences within groups of children as they age. For example, factors related to school and family were related to 11–17 year old youths' life satisfaction, but this correlation was weaker for the older youths (Karademas et al. 2008).

The differences in predictors of well-being for children and adults can be quite nuanced as when the variables related to income and religions are considered. There is now a substantial literature on the relationship between well-being, income, and wealth. Research has shown that, in general, people living in more wealthy nations are markedly happier than those living in relatively poor nations (Diener and Biswas-Diener 2002 for a review). This positive correlation between wealth and happiness is demonstrated within countries as well, though the strength of the correlation is typically weaker. The relationship between income and happiness is more nuanced than this summary suggests. For example, the strength of the relationship between income and well-being depends on the type of well-being considered. Income, and changes in one's income, is more strongly associated with life evaluations than with feelings of happiness (Diener et al. 2009, 2010).

Studies of the interrelationships between well-being, income, and wealth often have samples that are impressive in both their size and breadth. For instance, Diener et al. (2010) started with a sample of over 136,000 respondents from 132 countries. Most of these studies focus on adults, and few focus on preadolescent children. In the Diener et al. (2010) study, the youngest respondents were 15 years old. Findings from the few studies that do assess children do not indicate that increased household income is related to children's well-being. For example, our research group asked 8–12-year-old children and their parents to independently estimate their family's income (Holder and Coleman 2008). These two measures were positively correlated, suggesting that children are knowledgeable and aware of their family's income. Additionally, family income, either estimated by the children or the parents, correlated positively with the children's happiness. However, family income, either estimated by the children or reported by their parents, only explained 2–4% of the children's self-reported happiness and was not a significant predictor of children's happiness estimated by their parents, or teachers. In short, children were cognizant of the economic affluence of their household, but this affluence or lack thereof was not a strong predictor of their happiness.

In a study of 6th, 8th, 10th, and 12th graders using the Experience Sampling Method, the relationship between wealth and happiness clearly differed from that observed in adults (Csikszentmihalyi and Hunter 2003). When the youth and children were categorized into one of five groups based on family affluence, the second lowest class (i.e., "working class") reported the highest level of happiness and the two highest classes (i.e., "upper class" and "upper middle" class) reported the lowest levels of happiness. In fact, the lowest class which was the poor, reported more happiness than the upper class and the upper middle class.

There are several obvious differences between the studies described in the previous two paragraphs. The study conducted by Csikszentmihalyi and Hunter (2003), and the study by Holder and Coleman (2008) show dissimilar results, methods, and samples. Two differences are found in the methods used (experience sampling versus self-report questionnaires), and the age of participants (Grades 6–12 versus Grades 4–7). The discrepant results of these two studies may also be attributable to two less obvious, hidden, differences. First, the sample employed by Csikszentmihalyi and Hunter may have been broader as it was selected to be representative of variations in the labor force. The study by Holder and Coleman was not primarily focused on wealth, and the sample was selected from several different schools, but all were from a relatively affluent area of Canada. Perhaps the income range was somewhat truncated, thus obscuring a negative relationship between happiness and affluence. A second difference is that Csikszentmihalyi and Hunter assessed affluence at the community level, not at the level of individual households, as did Holder and Coleman (2008). This certainly may have led to the inconsistent results between the two studies.

Another exception to the summary statement that the correlates of children's and adults' positive well-being are similar is found in the details of the relationship between personality and happiness. As previously discussed, in general, the personality traits of adults have their early core counterparts in the temperament traits of children. Shiner (1998) reported that the Big Five personality dimensions that are widely accepted and studied in adults had parallel dimensions in measures of children's temperament. Shiner (1998) also noted that children's temperament is comprised of two additional factors, including one marked by high activity. Holder and Klassen (2010) reported that the temperament trait of activity was a significant positive predictor of happiness in children. However, the childhood trait of activity has no direct counterpart in adult personality. This provides another reason why it is important to study happiness specifically in children.

The fact that the trait of activity is not considered part of adults' personality may not pose a significant problem. The trait of activity is related to the personality trait of extraversion (DeNeve and Cooper 1998), and as described above, extraversion is a strong predictor of adults' happiness. Children with high levels of the temperament trait of activity show increased frequency of engaging in, preference for, and duration spent in high-energy activities (Buss and Plomin 1984). Thus, perhaps the high positive correlation between happiness and the trait of activity, observed in children, is related to the increase in vigorous physical activity. Results from a longitudinal study of adolescents are consistent with this understanding in that positive affect was higher during participation in physical activities, compared to simply resting (Weinstein and Mermelstein 2007). The evidence shows that engaging in physical activity is positively correlated with happiness in children, adolescents, and adults. In addition, the traits of activity and extraversion are positively correlated with engaging in physical activity and with each other. Although there is a difference between adults and children in predictors of happiness related to personality/temperament traits, it may be a function of the constructs, as they are currently understood. Regardless, future research is needed to clarify this relationship.

In addition to differences in the relationship between children's temperament and their happiness, and adults' personality and their happiness, there are differences between children and adults in the contributions of religiousness and spirituality to well-being. In general, adults who engage in more religious activity are slightly happier than those who participate in less (Arygle 2001). This positive correlation was supported by a literature review that concluded that the dimensions of spirituality and religiousness, including church attendance, were positively associated with happiness for adults (Francis et al. 2003). However, not all research has shown a positive relationship between happiness and spirituality and religiousness (Francis et al. 2003; Lewis 2002; Lewis et al. 1997, 2000). Based on a review of the literature, Lewis (2002) concluded that whether or not a study identifies an association between well-being and religiousness may be attributable to which measures of well-being the study employs. Therefore, the choice of measurement in a study can create a possible bias in the results.

A recent study of the relationship between children's happiness and their spirituality and religious practices reported results that differed in two main ways from those typically found with adults (Holder et al. 2010). First, the strength of the relationship between happiness and spirituality in children was stronger than that typically reported in adults. Up to 26% of the variance in children's happiness was explained by their spirituality, while in adults, spirituality typically accounts for 4–5% of the variance in happiness. This apparent difference may be misleading because some studies conducted with adults have methodological limitations that were not present in the study with children. For example, the range of individuals in Lewis et al. (2000) sample was severely restricted and therefore not representative of the wider community; only Anglican priests and members of the Anglican Church participated in their studies. Two additional factors may be further complicating the matter (Francis et al. 2003; Lewis 2002; Lewis et al. 2000). First there is no consensus amongst researchers as to the best measures of spirituality and religiousness. Second, many of the measures that are employed do not assess the constructs of spirituality and religiousness comprehensively; instead they assess the constructs from a more narrow Christian-only perspective.

Another difference between predictors of well-being in adults and children involves religious practice. For adults, positive correlations are found between weekly participation in public religious activity and well-being (Maselko and Kubzansky 2006), religious practice and happiness (Francis et al. 2003), and church attendance and overall life satisfaction (Ellison et al. 2001). For children, happiness and religious practice are *negatively*, though weakly, correlated (Holder et al. 2010). Perhaps the reported difference between adult's and children's well-being as it relates to religious activity is attributable to differences in the degree of choice. Children's participation in religious practices may not reflect their free choice. Parents may largely determine the place, frequency, and duration of children's religious practices, whereas adults may have more freedom of choice. This is similar to the issue discussed earlier regarding how children's choice of leisure pursuits may be limited. However, church attendance is also a poor predictor of happiness in groups believed, or known, to have more control over their personal religious practices. In one study, church attendance did not predict adolescents' life-satisfaction, whether or not they identified with a religious denomination (Kelley and Miller 2007), and in another, it was not positively related to the well-being of graduate students (Ciarrocchi and Deneke 2005). Although one might argue that many adolescents must still abide by many of their parents' decisions, and thus, many adolescents lack a true choice when it comes to attending a place of worship, graduate students, who are adults, likely make that choice voluntarily. Whether children experience a decrease in happiness because they lack the ability to choose religious practices for themselves is unknown. Also, which religious services to attend, how frequently, for how long, or factors related to the nature of the religious services themselves, are other possible factors in well-being that still need to be studied.

References

Amato, P. R. (1994). Father-child relations, mother-child relations, and offspring psychological well-being in early adulthood. *Journal of Marriage and the Family, 56*, 1031–1043.

Amato, P. R. (2006). Marital discord, divorce, and children's well-being: Results from a 20 year longitudinal study of two generations. In A. Clarke-Stewart & J. Dunn (Eds.), *Families count: Effects on child and adolescent development* (pp. 179–202). NY: Cambridge University Press.

Amato, P. R., & Afifi, T. D. (2006). Feeling caught between parents: Adult children's relations with parents and subjective well-being. *Journal of Marriage and Family, 68*, 222–235.

Amato, P. R., & Sobolewski, J. M. (2001). The effects of divorce and marital discord on adult children's psychological well-being. *American Sociological Review, 66*, 900–921.

Argyle, M. (2001). *The psychology of happiness* (2nd ed.). East Sussex: Routledge.

Argyle, M., & Lu, L. (1990). Happiness and social skills. *Personality and Individual Differences, 11*, 1255–1261.

Baird, B. M., Lucas, R. E., & Donnellan, M. B. (2010). Life satisfaction across the lifespan: Findings from two nationally representative panel studies. *Social Indicators Research, 99*, 183–203.

Belsky, J., Fish, M., & Isabella, R. (1991). Continuity and discontinuity in infant negative and positive emotionality: Family antecedents and attachment consequences. *Developmental Psychology, 27*, 421–431.

Belsky, J., Hsieh, K. H., & Crnic, K. (1996). Infant positive and negative emotionality: One dimension or two? *Developmental Psychology, 32*, 289–298.

Buss, A. H., & Plomin, R. (1984). *Temperament: Early developing personality traits*. New Jersey: Lawrence Erlbaum Associates, Hillsdale.

Caldwell, L. L. (2005). Leisure and health: Why is leisure therapeutic? *British Journal of Guidance and Counselling, 33*, 7–26.

Chaplin, L. N. (2009). Please may I have a bike? Better yet, may I have a hug? An examination of children's and adolescents' happiness. *Journal of Happiness Studies, 10*, 541–562.

Charles, S. T., Reynolds, C. A., & Gatz, M. (2001). Age related differences and change in positive and negative affect over 23 years. *Journal of Personality and Social Psychology, 80*, 136–151.

Cheng, H., & Furnham, A. (2001). Attributional style and personality as predictors of happiness and mental health. *Journal of Happiness Studies, 2*, 307–327.

Cheng, H., & Furnham, A. (2003). Personality, self-esteem, and demographic predictions of happiness and depression. *Personality and Individual Differences, 34*, 921–942.

Ciarrocchi, J. W., & Deneke, E. (2005). Happiness and the varieties of religious experience: Religious support, practices, and spirituality as predictors of well-being. *Research in the Social Scientific Study of Religion, 15*, 209–233.

Clifford, M. M., & Walster, E. (1973). Research note: The effects of physical attractiveness on teacher expectations. *Sociology of Education, 46*, 248–258.

Cohen, A. B. (2002). The importance of spirituality in well-being for Jews and Christians. *Journal of Happiness Studies, 3*, 287–310.

Costa, P. T., & McCrae, R. R. (1994). Stability and change in personality from adolescence through adulthood. In C. F. Halverson Jr, G. A. Kohnstamm, & R. P. Martin (Eds.), *The developing structure of temperament and personality from infancy to adulthood* (pp. 139–150). Hillsdale: Lawrence Erlbaum Assoc Inc.

Crossley, A., & Langdridge, D. (2005). Perceived sources of happiness: A network analysis. *Journal of Happiness Studies, 6*, 107–135.

Csikszentmihalyi, M., & Hunter, J. (2003). Happiness in everyday life: The uses of experience sampling. *Journal of Happiness Studies, 4*, 185–199.

Csikszentmihalyi, M., & LeFevre, J. (1989). Optimal experience in work and leisure. *Journal of Personality and Social Psychology, 56*, 815–822.

Deci, E. L., & Ryan, R. M. (1985a). *Intrinsic motivation and self-determination in human behavior.* NY: Plenum.

Deci, E. L., & Ryan, R. M. (1985b). The "what" and "why" of goal pursuits: Human needs and the self-determination of behavior. *Psychological Inquiry, 11,* 227–268.

Demir, M., & Weitekamp, L. A. (2006). I am so happy cause today I found my friend: Friendship and personality and predictors of happiness. *Journal of Happiness Studies, 8,* 181–211.

DeNeve, K. M., & Cooper, H. (1998). The happy personality: A meta-analysis of 137 personality traits and subjective well-being. *Psychological Bulletin, 124,* 197–229.

Diener, E., & Biswas-Diener, R. (2002). Will money increase subjective well-being? *Social Indicators Research, 57,* 119–169.

Diener, E., Diener, M., & Diener, C. (1995a). Factors predicting the subjective well being of nations. *Journal of Personality and Social Psychology, 69,* 851–864.

Diener, E., Kahneman, D., Tov, W., & Arora, R. (2009). Income's association with judgments of life versus feelings. In E. Diener, D. Kahneman, & J. F. Helliwell (Eds.), *International differences in well-being* (pp. 3–15). Oxford United Kingdom: Oxford University Press.

Diener, E., Ng, W., Harter, J., & Arora, R. (2010). Wealth and happiness across the world: Material prosperity predicts life evaluation, whereas psychosocial prosperity predicts positive feeling. *Journal of Personality and Social Psychology, 99,* 52–61.

Diener, E., Wolsic, B., & Fujita, F. (1995b). Physical attractiveness and subjective well-being. *Journal of Personality and Social Psychology, 34,* 7–32.

Eccles, J. S., Barber, B. L., Stone, M., & Hunt, J. (2003). Extracurricular activities and adolescent development. *Journal of Social Issues, 59,* 865–889.

Ellison, C. G. (1991). Religious involvement and subjective well-being. *Journal of Health and Social Behaviour, 32,* 80–99.

Ellison, C. G., Boardman, J., Williams, D. R., & Jackson, J. (2001). Religious involvement, stress, and mental health: Findings from the 1995 Detroit area study. *Social Forces, 80,* 215–249.

Feingold, A. (1992). Good-looking people are not what we think. *Psychological Bulletin, 111,* 304–341.

Field, T., Diego, M., & Sanders, C. E. (2001). Adolescent suicidal ideation. *Adolescence, 36,* 795–802.

Flouri, E., & Buchanan, A. (2003). The role of father involvement in children's later mental health. *Journal of Adolescence, 26,* 63–78.

Francis, L. J., Brown, L. B., Lester, D., & Philipchalk, R. (1998). Happiness as stable extraversion: A cross-cultural examination of the reliability and validity of the Oxford happiness inventory among students in the U.K., U.S.A., Australia, and Canada. *Personality and Individual Differences, 24,* 167–171.

Francis, L. J., Ziebertz, H., & Lewis, C. A. (2003). The relationship between religion and happiness among German students. *Pastoral Psychology, 51,* 273–281.

Frederick-Recascino, C. M., & Schuster-Smith, H. (2003). Competition and intrinsic motivation in physical activity: A comparison of two groups. *Journal of Sport Behavior, 26*(3), 240–254.

Frey, B. S., Benesch, C., & Stutzer, A. (2007). Does watching TV make us happy? *Journal of Economic Psychology, 28,* 283–313.

Gilbert, D., & Abdullah, J. (2004). Holiday taking and the sense of well-being. *Annals of Tourism Research, 31,* 103–121.

Gray, J. A. (1991). Neural systems, emotion, and personality. In J. Madden IV (Ed.), *Neurobiology and learning, emotion, and affect* (pp. 273–306). NY: Raven Press.

Grossman, M., & Rowat, K. M. (1995). Parental relationships, coping strategies, received support, and well-being in adolescents of separated or divorced and married parents. *Research in Nursing and Health, 18,* 249–261.

Gutriérrez, J. L. G., Jiménez, B. M., Hernández, E. G., & Puente, C. P. (2005). Personality and subjective well-being: Big five correlates and demographic variables. *Personality and Individual Differences, 38,* 1561–1569.

Hills, P., & Argyle, M. (1998). Positive moods derived from leisure and their relationship to happiness and personality. *Personality and Individual Differences, 25*, 523–535.

Heo, J., Kim, J., & Won, Y.-S. (2011). Exploring the relationship between internet use and leisure satisfaction among older adults. *Activities, Adaptation, and Aging, 35*, 43–54.

Holder, M. D., & Coleman, B. (2008). The contribution of temperament, popularity, and physical appearance to children's happiness. *Journal of Happiness Studies, 9*, 279–302.

Holder, M. D., & Coleman, B. (2009). The contribution of social relationships to children's happiness. *Journal of Happiness Studies, 10*, 329–349.

Holder, M. D., Coleman, B., & Sehn, Z. (2009). The contribution of active and passive leisure to children's well-being. *Journal of Health Psychology, 14*, 378–386.

Holder, M. D., Coleman, B., & Wallace, J. M. (2010). Spirituality, religiousness, and happiness in children aged 8–12 years. *Journal of Happiness Studies, 11*, 131–150.

Holder, M. D., & Klassen, A. (2010). Temperament and happiness in children. *Journal of Happiness Studies, 11*, 419–439.

Huebner, E. S. (1991). Correlates of life satisfaction in children. *School Psychology Quarterly, 6*, 103–111.

Karademas, E. C., Peppa, N., Fotiou, A., & Kokkevi, A. (2008). Family, school and health in children and adolescents: Findings from the 2006 HBSC study in Greece. *Journal of Health Psychology, 13*(8), 1012–1020.

Kasser, T., & Ahuvia, A. (2002). Materialistic values and well-being in business students. *European Journal of Social Psychology, 32*, 137–146.

Kelley, B. S., & Miller, L. (2007). Life satisfaction and spirituality in adolescents. *Research in the Social Scientific Study of Religion, 18*, 233–262.

Kohler, H. (2005). Attitudes and low fertility: Reflections based on Danish twin data. In A. Booth & A. C. Crouter (Eds.), *The new population problem: Why families in developed countries are shrinking and what it means* (pp. 99–113). Mahwah: Lawrence Erlbaum Associates Publishers.

Larsen, R. J., & Rusting, C. L. (1997). Extraversion, neuroticism, and susceptibility to positive and negative affect: A test of two theoretical models. *Personality and Individual Differences, 22*, 607–612.

Lewis, A. L. (2002). Church attendance and happiness among Northern Irish undergraduate students: No association. *Pastoral Psychology, 50*, 191–195.

Lewis, C. A., Lanigan, C., Joseph, S., & de Fockert, J. (1997). Religiosity and happiness: No evidence for an association among undergraduates. *Personality and Individual Differences, 22*, 119–121.

Lewis, C. A., Maltby, J., & Burkinshaw, S. (2000). Religion and happiness: Still no association. *Journal of Beliefs and Values, 21*, 233–236.

Lu, L., & Hu, C. (2005). Personality, leisure experiences and happiness. *Journal of Happiness Studies, 6*, 325–342.

Lu, L., & Lin, Y. Y. (1998). Family roles and happiness in adulthood. *Personality and Individual Differences, 25*, 195–207.

Lucas, R. E., & Diener, E. (2001). Understanding extraverts' enjoyment of social situations: The importance of pleasantness. *Journal of Personality and Social Psychology, 81*, 343–356.

Lyubomirsky, S., King, L., & Diener, E. (2005). The benefits of frequent positive affect: Does happiness lead to success? *Psychological Bulletin, 131*, 803–855.

Maselko, J., & Kubzansky, L. D. (2006). Gender differences in religious practices, spiritual experiences and health: Results from the US general social survey. *Social Science and Medicine, 62*, 2848–2860.

McKnight, C. G., Huebner, E. S., & Suldo, S. (2002). Relationships among stressful life events, temperament, problem behavior, and global life satisfaction in adolescents. *Psychology in the Schools, 39*, 677–687.

Meyer, B., Enström, M. K., Harstveit, M., Bowles, D. P., & Beevers, C. G. (2007). Happiness and despair on the catwalk: Need satisfaction, well-being, and personality adjustment among fashion models. *The Journal of Positive Psychology, 2*, 2–17.

Moxnes, K. (2003). Risk factors in divorce: Perceptions by the children involved. *Childhood: A Global Journal of Child Research, 10*, 131–146.

Mroczek, D. K., & Alameida, D. M. (2004). The effects of daily stress, age and personality on daily negative affect. *Journal of Personality, 72*, 354–378.

Mroczek, D. K., & Spiro, A., I. I. I. (2005). Change in life satisfaction during adulthood: Findings from the veterans affairs normative aging study. *Journal of Personality and Social Psychology, 88*, 189–202.

Neto, F. (2001). Personality predictors of happiness. *Psychological Reports, 88*, 817–824.

Onishi, J., Masuda, Y., Suzuki, Y., Gotoh, T., Kawamura, T., & Iguchi, A. (2006). The pleasurable recreational activities among community-dwelling older adults. *Archives of Gerontology and Geriatrics, 43*, 147–155.

Ostberg, V. (2003). Children in classrooms: Peer status, status distribution and mental well-being. *Social Science and Medicine, 56*, 17–29.

Otake, K., Shimai, S., & Tanaka-Matsumi, J. (2006). Happy people become happier through kindness: A counting kindness intervention. *Journal of Happiness Studies, 7*, 361–375.

Parfitt, G., & Eston, R. G. (2005). The relationship between children's habitual activity level and psychological well-being. *Acta Paediatrica, 94*, 1791–1797.

Pinquart, M., & Sorensen, S. (2001). Gender differences in self-concept and psychological well-being in old age: A meta-analysis. *Journal of Gerontology, 56B*, 195–213.

Reich, J. W., & Zautra, A. (1981). Life events and personal causation: Some relationships with satisfaction and distress. *Journal of Personality and Social Psychology, 41*, 1002–1012.

Rodgers, B., Power, C., & Hope, S. (1997). Parental divorce and adult psychological distress: Evidence from a national cohort: A research note. *Journal of Child Psychology and Psychiatry, 38*, 867–872.

Ryan, R. M., & Deci, E. L. (2000). Self-determination theory and the facilitation of intrinsic motivation, social development, and well-being. *American Psychologist, 55*, 68–78.

Sacker, A., & Cable, N. (2006). Do adolescent leisure-time physical activities foster health and well-being in adulthood? Evidence from two British birth cohorts. *European Journal of Public Health, 16*, 331–335.

Schimmack, U., Oishi, S., & Diener, E. (2002). Cultural influences on the relation between pleasant emotions and unpleasant emotions: Asian dialectic philosophies or individualism-collectivism? *Cognition and Emotion, 16*, 705–719.

Searle, M. S., Mahon, M. J., Iso-Ahola, S. E., Sdrolias, H. A., & van Dyck, J. (1998). Examining the long term effects of leisure education on a sense of independence and psychological well-being among the elderly. *Journal of Leisure Research, 30*, 331–340.

Shaw, L. H., & Gant, L. M. (2002). Users divided? exploring the gender gap in internet use. *Cyber Psychology and Behavior, 5*, 517–527.

Shiner, R. L. (1998). How shall we speak of children's personalities in middle childhood? A preliminary taxonomy. *Psychological Bulletin, 124*, 308–332.

Shiner, R., & Caspi, A. (2003). Personality differences in childhood and adolescence: Measurement, development and consequences. *Journal of Child Psychology and Psychiatry, 44*, 2–32.

Slee, P. T. (1993). Australian school children' self appraisal of interpersonal relations. The bullying experience. *Child Psychiatry and Human Development, 23*, 273–282.

Steel, P., Schmidt, J., & Shultz, J. (2008). Refining the relationship between personality and subjective well-being. *Psychological Bulletin, 134*, 138–161.

Stokes, R., & Frederick-Recascino, C. (2003). Women's perceived body image: Relations with personal happiness. *Journal of Women and Aging, 15*, 17–29.

Stones, M. J., Worobetz, S., & Brink, P. (2011). Overestimated relationships with subjective well-being. *Canadian Psychology, 52*, 93–100.

Tedeschi, R. G., & Calhoun, L. G. (1995). *Trauma and transformation: Growing in the aftermath of suffering*. Thousand Oaks: Sage.

Tedeschi, R. G., & Calhoun, L. G. (2004). Post-traumatic growth: Conceptual foundations and empirical evidence. *Psychological Inquiry, 15*, 1–18.

Tedeschi, R. G., Park, C. L., & Calhoun, L. G. (Eds.). (1998). *Post-traumatic growth: Positive changes in the aftermath of crisis.* Mahwah: Lawrence Erlbaum.

Umberson, D., & Hughes, M. (1987). The impact of physical attractiveness on achievement and psychological well-being. *Social Psychology Quarterly, 50,* 227–236.

Ussher, M. H., Owen, C. G., Cook, D. G., & Whincup, P. H. (2007). The relationship between physical activity, sedentary behavior and psychological wellbeing among adolescents. *Social Psychiatry and Psychiatric Epidemiology, 42,* 851–856.

Uusitalo-Malmivaara, L. (in press). Global and school-related happiness in finnish children. *Journal of Happiness Studies.*

Vandell, D. L., Shernoff, D. J., Pierce, K. M., Bolt, D. M., Dadisman, K., & Brown, B. B. (2005). Activities, engagement, and emotion in after-school programs (and elsewhere). *New Directions for Youth Development, 105,* 121–129.

Vella-Brodrick, D. A., & Freire, T. (2011). *Differences in well-being ratings for individuals with electronic based hobbies compared to those with non-electronic hobbies.* Paper presented at the 2nd World Congress on Positive Psychology, Philadelphia, USA.

Weinstein, S. M., & Mermelstein, R. (2007). Relations between daily activities and adolescent mood: The role of autonomy. *Journal of Clinical and Adolescent Psychology, 36,* 182–194.

Chapter 6
Application of Theory to Positive Well-Being in Children

The identification by researchers of many of the correlates of well-being has contributed to theories of subjective well-being and its components. Positive psychology has now matured to the point where several theories have been developed to help understand the experience and benefits of positive well-being. These theories have been used to predict why certain proposed interventions should, and should not, be undertaken. They also help to explain why specific exercises do, and do not, increase levels of well-being. It is beyond the scope of the present work to present a comprehensive review of the current theories in positive psychology. However, this section selectively reviews a few theories to demonstrate that even though these theories have not always been applied to and tested with children, they hold promise in their potential to explain well-being in children.

In general, many influential theories in positive psychology have neither been extensively applied to nor directly tested with children. For instance, in Fredrickson's influential Broaden and Build Theory of positive emotions, emotions such as happiness and joy contribute a broadening of one's awareness and attention (Fredrickson 2001). This broadening serves to support a wider range of cognitive and behavioral activity. The more one engages in this broadening of thoughts and actions, the more one builds up skills and resources to more successfully cope with the vicissitudes of life. This broadening and building of positive emotions is in contrast to the theorized role of negative emotions. Negative emotions, such as anxiety, serve to narrow and focus attention on behaviors that promote immediate survival (e.g., fight or flight), instead of long-term happiness.

The Broaden and Build theory would seem to be particularly applicable to children. Children's lives are characterized by developing skills and resources to more effectively interact with their environment. Ideally, childhood corresponds to a time of life that is ripe with creative thinking and learning (i.e., the broadening component of the theory). A successful childhood is characterized by development and improvement in the child's long-term resources, including those related to relationships, skills, and overall health (i.e., the build component of the theory). However, despite what seems like a valuable extension of this influential theory, researchers have not yet applied much effort to extending this theory to children and their positive emotions.

Another major theory that has played an important role in the thinking and research of positive psychology involves the role of optimal experience (Csikszentmihalyi 1990). This experience, known as flow, is when individuals experience a state where they are absorbed with an intrinsically motivated activity, such that they lose track of time. This state occurs when one is fully concentrating, such as when a challenging task is complemented by one's ability to successfully meet the challenge. Experiencing flow involves feelings of absorption, engagement, fulfillment, happiness, and satisfaction. Flow and the benefits derived from the phenomenon have been demonstrated in a wide range of people including across cultures (Delle Fave et al. 2011), and across ages from adolescents (Seifert and Hedderson 2010) to the elderly (Collins et al. 2009).

However, the role of flow in children has not received much attention from researchers. The lack of research on flow in children is unfortunate. Educators and parents could likely benefit from empirical findings that may demonstrate both the immediate and enduring benefits from flow, and suggest ways to allow children to recognize and experience it. Adults are more likely to experience flow at work than at home (Csikszentmihalyi and LeFevre 1989). Perhaps children are more likely to experience flow at school, in which case it would be a good environment for research to investigate flow in children. Two recent studies have investigated this possibility. In the first study, a boy experienced flow while learning to write in a classroom (Bowles 2009). In the second study, children with adjustment difficulties experienced flow during art-making sessions (Lee 2010). These studies are promising as they suggest that children do experience and benefit from flow in the classroom. However, these studies are limited in that they only studied nine children in total.

The Broaden and Build theory and theories of flow represent only a small sample of the number of theories now developed in positive psychology. Many additional theories should be valuable in understanding well-being in children. For instance, Self-Discrepancy Theory posits that well-being is enhanced by reducing the discrepancy between the actual self and the ideal self (Higgins 1987). Applying this theory to well-being suggests that interventions may enhance well-being by drawing attention to characteristics of an ideal self (e.g., engaging in acts of kindness) or instructing the participant to engage in behaviors that emulate his or her ideal self (i.e., helping someone in need). As a result, these interventions may enhance well-being by helping to reduce the discrepancy between and individual's actual and ideal self. This theory could be applied to children and suggests interventions that incorporate the interests of children such as video games. In fact, the research shows that the appeal of video games may be enhanced when, within a game, you are able to act more like your ideal self (Przybylski et al. 2012).

Alternatively, Adaptation Theory and its more recent revisions suggest that well-being undergoes a process similar to habituation (Diener et al. 2006).

According to this theory, interventions may be more successful if they help participants savor positive aspects of life, which in turn can mitigate the adaptation that may limit increases to well-being (Bryant and Veroff 2007). Therefore, interventions designed to enhance well-being in children may be successful if these interventions interfere with this adaptation. Other theories claim that well-being is enhanced by engaging in behaviors (e.g., performing acts of kindness) that cultivate virtues and lead us to attaining our full potential (Ryff 1989; Waterman 1993). Therefore, interventions that prompt children to engage in virtuous acts may elevate well-being. Related to this are evolutionary-based theories of well-being (Keltner 2009) which postulate that our capacity for good is biologically prewired, and interventions can enhance well-being because they are consistent with our genetic predispositions.

References

Bowles, P. H. (2009). A case study of a first-grade boy's writing flow: when creativity and the discipline of work connect. *Dissertation Abstracts International Section A: Humanities and Social Sciences.* 69(7-A), 2599.

Bryant, F. B., & Veroff, J. (2007). *Savoring: a new model of positive experience.* Mahwah: Lawrence Erlbaum Associates Publishers.

Collins, A. L., Sarkisian, N., & Winner, E. (2009). Flow and happiness in later life: an investigation into the role of daily and weekly flow experiences. *Journal of Happiness Studies, 10,* 703–719.

Csikszentmihalyi, M. (1990). *Flow: The psychology of optimal experience.* NY: Harper.

Csikszentmihalyi, M., & LeFevre, J. (1989). Optimal experience in work and leisure. *Journal of Personality and Social Psychology, 56,* 815–822.

Delle Fave, A., Massimini, F., & Bassi, M. (2011). *Psychological selection and optimal experience across cultures: Social empowerment through personal growth. Cross-cultural advancements in positive psychology.* NY: Springer.

Diener, E., Lucas, R. E., & Scollon, C. N. (2006). Beyond the hedonic treadmill: revising the adaptation theory of well-being. *American Psychologist, 61,* 305–314.

Fredrickson, B. L. (2001). The role of positive emotions in positive psychology: the broaden-and-build theory of positive emotions. *American Psychologist, 56,* 218–226.

Higgins, E. T. (1987). Self-discrepancy theory: a theory relating self and affect. *Psychological Review, 94,* 319–340.

Keltner, D. (2009). *Born to be good: The science of a meaningful life.* NY: W. W. Norton & Co.

Lee, S. Y. (2010). The experience of 'flow' in artistic expression: case studies of immigrant Korean children with adjustment difficulties. *Dissertation Abstracts International Section A: Humanities and Social Sciences.* 70(7-A), 2344.

Przybylski, A. K., Weinstein, N., Murayama, K., Lynch, M. F., & Ryan, R. M. (2012). The ideal self at play: The appeal of videogames that let you be all you can be. *Psychological Science, 23,* 69–76.

Seifert, T., & Hedderson, C. (2010). Intrinsic motivation and flow in skateboarding: an ethnographic study. *Journal of Happiness Studies, 11,* 277–292.

Ryff, C. D. (1989). Happiness is everything, or is it? Explorations on the meaning of psychological well-being. *Journal of Personality and Social Psychology, 57,* 1069–1081.

Waterman, A. S. (1993). Two conceptions of happiness: contrasts of personal expressiveness (eudaimonia) and hedonic enjoyment. *Journal of Personality and Social Psychology, 64,* 678–691.

Chapter 7
Individual Differences

Though it is tempting to think that theories in positive psychology can lead to interventions that will promote well-being in all children, this is almost certainly not the case. Researchers in a relatively new field, such as the study of children in positive psychology, are sometimes prone to overgeneralizing their results. This may be related to the initial lack of research that considers the full breadth of individual differences. As a field matures, individual differences are more closely examined, resulting in a finer grain set of conclusions and more nuanced theories. It is a process that is akin to the old adage "Today's truths become tomorrow's exceptions." Culture is an example of an important source of individual differences in the study of children's strengths that researchers have only recently started to consider.

Culture: Though studies have begun to identify the relationships between a host of variables and children's subjective positive well-being, any global conclusions we can reach are only tentative. One important reason for this is that many studies draw their samples of children from a primarily western industrialized population, and therefore also from individualistic cultures. In the study of temperament in children, Huebner (1991) completed important work demonstrating that temperament traits related to the adult personality trait of extraversion were positively correlated with life satisfaction. Furthermore, he reported that temperament traits related to neuroticism were negatively correlated with life satisfaction. These associations were later demonstrated in samples of older children (Grades 6–12) (McKnight et al. 2002). More recently, Holder and Klassen (2010) found similar results for the relationships between temperament and happiness in 9–12 year old children; temperament traits related to extraversion were positively correlated with happiness and traits related to neuroticism were negatively correlated with happiness. However, research from these studies only assessed well-being and temperament in children living in North America (i.e., Midwest, South Carolina, and Western Canada). Though a substantial literature on similarities and differences in adult personality across cultures is now established, few studies have assessed cross-cultural differences in children's temperament (Shiner and Caspi 2003).

Research suggests that restricting the samples to only a few similar cultures may limit the generalizability of the findings in important ways. This limitation may be of a particular concern regarding the relationship between well-being and temperament. Many research findings, including those related to personality and well-being, are sensitive to cultural variation. For example, self-rated personality traits of citizens from the Philippines, a collectivist culture, differed from self-rated traits from citizens of North America, where cultures are primarily individualistic (Grimm et al. 1999). Additionally, research has reported cultural differences in well-being. For instance, life satisfaction was greater in the USA than Germany, and greater in Germany than Turkey (McConatha et al. 2004). Cultural differences in well-being are persistent. Differences in well-being attributable to culture are maintained across generations even after an individual immigrates to a different continent (Rice and Steele 2004; Veenhoven 1994).

In addition, research suggests that there are cross-cultural differences in the appropriate contexts of expression and comprehension of emotions, including those linked to well-being. For example, the expression of happiness is accepted by Americans as more appropriate in a broader range of contexts than it is for Japanese (Matsumoto 2000). Additionally, the construct of happiness varies between cultures. In the West, happiness is conceptualized as more closely linked to intrapersonal or internal assessment involving contentment. In China, happiness is conceptualized as a more interpersonal, or external assessment, involving satisfaction and it includes unique dimensions such as ease with life, not included in the West (Lu and Shih 1997). There are also cultural differences in happiness and unhappiness between Americans and Japanese (Uchida and Kitayama 2009). Americans associated the positive hedonic pleasure of happiness with individual achievement, whereas Japanese associated this component with social harmony. Additionally, Japanese were more likely to associate unhappiness with negative outcomes (e.g., social disruption) than Americans.

As a result of cross-cultural research, theorists have suggested that aspects of both well-being and personality are affected by culture (Aaker et al. 2001; Church 2000; Markus and Kitayama 1998). In fact, Kitayama and Markus (2000) suggest that the ways in which people conceptualize and experience well-being are culturally determined. This perspective is supported by research showing that the personality traits of immigrants become increasingly similar to citizens of their adopted nations, as the number of years they live in that country increases (McCrae et al. 1998).

Though cultural variation in personality and well-being exists, the Five-Factor model of personality applies to a wide range of different cultures (McCrae and Allik 2002; McCrae and Costa 1997; McCrae and Terracciano 2005). For instance, the Five-Factor model was successfully applied to a sample of adolescents in Taiwan (Wu et al. 2008). This finding supported the position that the Five-Factor model generalizes across countries and provides an example of its use in an Eastern, collectivistic culture. However, this does not mean that there are no differences in personality across different cultures. For example, though the overall personality profiles of people in different cultures may be explained by the Five-Factor model, the levels of each personality factor do differ across cultures (Schmitt et al. 2007).

To help address the concern that studies of the relationships between well-being and temperament in children are largely from a single culture, we repeated our earlier work (Holder and Klassen 2010) with children living in northern India (Holder et al. in press). Across raters (i.e., children and parents) and measures of well-being, temperament was correlated with happiness in Indian children. These correlations were similar, but not identical, to those reported using a Canadian sample of children (Holder and Klassen 2010). In terms of similarity, those children who were rated as more social, more active, and less shy were happier. Temperament characterized by high levels of sociability and low levels of shyness is related to the personality trait of extraversion (Buss and Plomin 1984). This finding is consistent with the adult literature showing a strong and consistent positive correlation between happiness and extraversion in adults (Steel et al. 2007). Therefore, results from the Indian sample of children paralleled the results from a Canadian sample of children as well as the adult literature, finding that extraversion is associated with happiness.

However, not all of the results from the Indian sample were consistent with the adult literature and the results obtained from a sample of Canadian children. Our earlier work with Canadian children showed that emotionality was significantly negatively correlated with happiness (Holder and Klassen 2010). With the Indian sample, emotionality was also negatively correlated with four different measures of happiness, but was only significant for one measure (i.e., children's self-reports using the Faces Scale). High levels of emotionality in children parallel the personality trait of neuroticism in adults (Buss and Plomin 1984). Of all the personality traits, neuroticism is one of the strongest and most consistent predictors of adult unhappiness (DeNeve and Cooper 1998; Steel et al. 2007).

In general, happiness in children from India was not as strongly predicted by temperament as was happiness in children from Canada. In the sample of Indian children, 4–11% of the variance in the four measures of happiness was predicted by children's temperaments. However, in our previous work based on the Canadian sample of children using very similar instruments and procedures, 9–29% of the variance in children's happiness was accounted for by their temperaments (Holder and Klassen 2010).

One simple, and perhaps less interesting explanation for the weaker association between happiness and temperament in the Indian sample is that the measures of happiness and/or temperament were less reliable and less valid in the Indian sample. Given that many of the parents and children in India did not use English as their first language, they may have had more difficulties with the assessments. Support for this possibility includes that we found that reliability estimates for the tests were lower for the Indian than the Canadian sample. However, this may not be the whole explanation. Weaker relationships between well-being and personality in adults have also been reported in Indian adults. In particular, one study examined the relationship between life satisfaction and the Big-five personality traits in an Indian sample of university students who should not have had difficulty with the English questionnaires employed (Singh 2007). The research showed that life satisfaction was positively correlated with extraversion, conscientiousness, and openness to experience (as is often found in North American and European samples of adults) but these personality traits only accounted for about 9% of the variance in life satisfaction. One can contrast the strength of this relationship with studies that rely on adults sampled from North American populations, which find that personality traits account for over half the variance of the adults' happiness (Demir and Weitekamp 2006).

Northern India was only one of the large number of possible populations from which to sample from. For several reasons it represented a particularly interesting opportunity to assess the generalizability of the associations between temperament and happiness that were found in North American children. First, Asians generally do not score as high as North Americans on extraversion (Allik and McCrae 2004; McCrae and Terracciano 2005), a trait strongly associated with well-being (Steel et al. 2008). Second, the large geographic distance between India and North America may be important because research based on people from 36 different cultures has found that personality traits are less similar as the distance between populations increases (Allik and McCrae 2004). Third, aspects of subjective well-being are known to differ between India and North America. In particular, citizens of India and North America differ in the importance they place on the degree to which one's actions result in personal pleasure (Rozin 1999). Finally, the spiritual and religious backgrounds and practices of North Americans and Indians are substantially different. The samples of children employed in the North American-based studies were probably predominantly Christian, whereas Christianity is adopted by only a small number of northern Indians. Cross-cultural differences in spirituality and religiosity may be important to research on positive well-being in children because spirituality was shown to predict levels of happiness in children aged 8–12 years (Holder et al. 2010).

Future studies should be sensitive to cultural differences, including differences in the degree to which a society can be characterized as collectivistic and individualistic, because these differences may influence the relationships between temperament and well-being. Though there are no studies that clearly disentangle the interactive roles of temperament, positive well-being, and collectivism/individualism in children, studies have shown that the relationships between personality and well-being in adults differ for different types of culture. For instance, the traits of extraversion and neuroticism were more strongly correlated with well-being in people from individualistic cultures than collectivist cultures (Schimmack et al. 2002). Research suggests that aspects of well-being, including life satisfaction, differ with the level of individualism and collectivism within and between cultures (Bennencourt and Dorr 1997; Diener et al. 1995; Schyns 1998). Additionally, the factors that predict life satisfaction are not the same between individualist and collectivist societies (Oishi et al. 1999) and people from individualistic cultures take into account their own satisfaction more often than people from collectivist cultures (Diener and Suh 1999).

References

Aaker, J., Benet-Martinez, V., & Garolera, J. (2001). Consumption symbols as carriers of culture: a study of Japanese and Spanish brand personality constructs. *Journal of Personality and Social Psychology, 81*, 249–264.

Allik, J., & McCrae, R. R. (2004). Toward a geography of personality traits: patterns of profiles across 36 cultures. *Journal of Cross-Cultural Psychology, 35*, 13–28.

Bennencourt, B. A., & Dorr, N. (1997). Collective self esteem as a mediator of the relationship between allocentrism and subjective well being. *Personality and Social Psychology Bulletin, 23*, 955–964.

Buss, A. H., & Plomin, R. (1984). *Temperament: Early developing personality traits*. Hillsdale: Lawrence Erlbaum Associates.

Church, A. T. (2000). Culture and personality: toward an integrated cultural trait psychology. *Journal of Personality, 68*, 651–703.

Demir, M., & Weitekamp, L. A. (2006). I am so happy cause today I found my friend: friendship and personality and predictors of happiness. *Journal of Happiness Studies, 8*, 181–211.

DeNeve, K. M., & Cooper, H. (1998). The happy personality: a meta-analysis of 137 personality traits and subjective well-being. *Psychological Bulletin, 124*, 197–229.

Diener, E., & Suh, E. M. (1999). National differences in subjective well being. In D. Kahneman, E. Diener, & N. Schwarz (Eds.), *Well being: The foundations of hedonic psychology* (pp. 434–450). New York: Russell Sage Foundation.

Diener, E., Diener, M., & Diener, C. (1995). Factors predicting the subjective well being of nations. *Journal of Personality and Social Psychology, 69*, 851–864.

Grimm, S. D., Church, A. T., Katigbak, M. S., & Reyes, J. A. S. (1999). Self described trait, values and moods associated with individualism and collectivism (I-C): testing I-C theory in an individualist (U.S.) and a collectivist (Philippines) culture. *Journal of Cross-Cultural Psychology, 30*, 466–500.

Holder, M. D., & Klassen, A. (2010). Temperament and happiness in children. *Journal of Happiness Studies, 11*, 419–439.

Holder, M. D., Coleman, B., & Wallace, J. M. (2010). Spirituality, religiousness, and happiness in children aged 8–12 years. *Journal of Happiness Studies, 11*, 131–150.

Holder, M. D., Coleman, B., & Singh, K. (in press). Temperament and happiness in children in India. *Journal of Happiness Studies*.

Huebner, E. S. (1991). Correlates of life satisfaction in children. *School Psychology Quarterly, 6*, 103–111.

Kitayama, S., & Markus, H. R. (2000). The pursuit of happiness and the realization of sympathy: cultural patterns of self, social relations, and well-being. In: Ed Diener & Eunkook M. Suh (Eds.), *Culture and subjective well-being* (pp. 113–161). Cambridge, MA, US: The MIT Press.

Lu, L., & Shih, J. B. (1997). Personality and happiness: Is mental health a mediator? *Personality and Individual Differences, 22*, 249–256.

Markus, H., & Kitayama, S. (1998). The cultural psychology of personality. *Journal of Cross Cultural Psychology, 29*, 119–149.

Matsumoto, D. (2000). *Culture and psychology: people around the world* (2nd ed.). Belmont CA: Wadsworth/Thomson Learning.

McConatha, J. T., Rieser-Danner, L., Harmer, K., Hayta, V., & Polat, T. S. (2004). Life satisfaction in three countries. *Psychological Reports, 94*, 795–806.

McCrae, R. R., & Allik, J. (Eds.). (2002). *The five factor model of personality across cultures*. New York: Kluwer Academic/Plenum Publishers.

McCrae, R. R., & Costa, P. T. (1997). Personality trait structure as a human universal. *American Psychologist, 52*, 509–516.

McCrae, R. R., & Terracciano, A. (2005). Personality profiles of cultures: aggregate personality traits. *Journal of Personality and Social Psychology, 89*, 407–425.

McCrae, R. R., Yik, S. S. M., Trapnell, P. D., Bond, M. H., & Paulhus, D. L. (1998). Interpreting personality profiles across cultures: bilingual acculturation and peer ratings of Chinese undergraduates. *Journal of Personality and Social Psychology, 74*, 1041–1055.

McKnight, C. G., Huebner, E. S., & Suldo, S. (2002). Relationships among stressful life events, temperament, problem behavior, and global life satisfaction in adolescents. *Psychology in the Schools, 39*, 677–687.

Oishi, S., Diener, E., Lucas, R. E., & Suh, E. (1999). Cross cultural variation in predictors of life satisfaction: perspectives from needs and values. *Personality and Social Psychology Bulletin, 25*, 980–990.

Rice, T. W., & Steele, B. J. (2004). Subjective well being and culture across time and space. *Journal of Cross Cultural Psychology, 35*, 633–647.

Rozin, P. (1999). Preadaptation and the puzzles of pleasure. In D. Kahneman, E. Diener, & N. Schwarz (Eds.), *Well being: The foundations of hedonic psychology* (pp. 109–133). New York: Russell Sage Foundation.

Schimmack, U., Radhakrishnan, P., Oishi, S., Dzokoto, V., & Ahadi, S. (2002). Culture, personality, and subjective well being: integrating process models of life satisfaction. *Journal of Personality and Social Psychology, 82*, 582–593.

Schmitt, D. P., Allik, J., Mccrae, R. R., & Benet-Martínez, V. (2007). The geographic distribution of big five personality traits: patterns and profiles of human self-description across 56 nations. *Journal of Cross-Cultural Psychology, 38*, 173–212.

Schyns, P. (1998). Cross national differences in happiness: economic and cultural factors explored. *Social Indicators Research, 43*, 3–26.

Shiner, R., & Caspi, A. (2003). Personality differences in childhood and adolescence: measurement, development and consequences. *Journal of Child Psychology and Psychiatry, 44*, 2–32.

Singh, K. (2007). Relationship between big five personality and constructs of Positive psychology. *Sutra: The Journal for Research on Education, Psychology, Traditional Sciences & Systems, Health and Consciousness, 1*, 129–137.

Steel, P., Schmidt, J., & Shultz, J. (2008). Refining the relationship between personality and subjective well-being. *Psychological Bulletin, 134*, 138–161.

Uchida, Y., & Kitayama, S. (2009). Happiness and unhappiness in east and west: themes and variations. *Emotion, 9*, 441–456.

Veenhoven, R. (1994). Is happiness and trait? Test of the theory that a better society does not make a person happy. *Social Indicators Research, 32*, 101–160.

Wu, K., Lindsted, K. D., Tsai, S., & Lee, J. W. (2008). Chinese NEO-PI-R in Taiwanese adolescents. *Personality and Individual Differences, 44*, 656–667.

Chapter 8
Are Children Happy?

Though several factors such as culture and temperament contribute to individual differences in the well-being of children, the current research supports one very positive conclusion. Studies that use self-reports and those that rely on other reports of children's happiness consistently report that children experience high levels of happiness. Several of our own studies that have investigated the happiness of 8 to 12 year-old children in Canada confirm this. Whether the children self-report their own happiness, or teachers or parents estimate the children's happiness, the results indicate that the large majority of children are happy. As mentioned earlier, we have used the Faces Scale to estimate happiness in children. The scale has seven faces to choose from and the midpoint, which represents a neutral face (i.e., neither happy nor sad), is the fourth face. In our research, about 90% of children rate themselves as being happier than the midpoint and their parents and teachers agree (Holder and Coleman 2008). These findings are consistent with studies of adults' happiness. For example, Myers (2000) reported that 90% of adult Americans self-reported that they were "pretty happy" or "very happy" and we have found that about 90% of the parents of the children we study rate themselves in one of the three happiest categories on the Faces Scale.

In addition to this encouraging finding, we found that very few children report that they are unhappy. Using the Faces Scale, we typically find that only 3% of children report that they are in the three least happy categories. However, one might consider that these results are not representative of children in general. After all, the children in several of our studies were sampled from a population characterized as wealthy relative to global standards, with excellent schooling and health care. Furthermore, they are from a country, Canada, which consistently rates high in terms of overall happiness. However, using similar procedures and the same measures, we obtained similar results with children aged 7–17 years of age in a sample from northern India (Holder et al. in press). In fact, the children in this sample rated themselves, and were rated by their parents, as slightly happier than the children in our Canadian sample. In the Indian sample, 94% of the

M. D. Holder, *Happiness in Children*, SpringerBriefs in Well-Being and Quality of Life Research, DOI: 10.1007/978-94-007-4414-1_8, © The Author(s) 2012

children rated themselves in the top three happiest categories of the Faces Scale and none of the children rated themselves in the three lowest categories of happiness. The children in this study from India were selected from within and around New Delhi. This region does not benefit from the economic opportunities associated with our earlier studies which used a sample of children from one of the wealthier areas of Canada.

These results do not support the perspective of Sigmund Freud who advocated that "Much has been gained if we succeed in turning your hysterical misery into common unhappiness." Research with adults has demonstrated that unhappiness is not common at all. Our studies of children suggest that unhappiness is rare in children as well.

References

Holder, M. D., & Coleman, B. (2008). The contribution of temperament, popularity, and physical appearance to children's happiness. *Journal of Happiness Studies, 9*, 279–302.

Holder, M. D., Coleman, B., & Singh, K. (in press). Temperament and happiness in children in India. *Journal of Happiness Studies*.

Myers, D. G. (2000). The funds, friends, and faith of happy people. *American Psychologist, 55*, 56–67.

Chapter 9
Enhancing Children's Well-Being

Though research suggests that children's well-being, or at least their happiness, is generally at a high level, this should not lead to complacency in positive psychology. There is still room to develop and test interventions that further promote the well-being of children. Though psychologists recognize that a substantial component of our positive subjective well-being, including our happiness, is governed by our genetic composition, we also recognize that a sizable component lies outside of our DNA and that we can select strategies that may influence our well-being. Furthermore, this influence may be relatively enduring. Using what we now know about children's well-being, researchers are developing and assessing programs designed to enhance children's well-being. Often these programs are implemented in schools and are grounded in the empirical and theoretical work of positive psychology. Two examples of these programs are highlighted here: the Penn Resiliency Program and Hope-Based Interventions.

Penn Resiliency Program: The Penn resiliency program is a cognitive-behavioral program typically administered to groups of youths ranging in age from 10 to 14 years old. This program is designed to achieve two goals: (1) assist students in identifying their signature character strengths and (2) enable students to employ these strengths in their everyday life. The Penn Resiliency Program has been typically evaluated on its ability to lower components of subjective negative well-being. A meta-analysis concluded that the program effectively reduces depressive symptoms, including at a 12-month follow-up, but the effects were modest (Brunwasser et al. 2009). Additionally, early reports suggest that the program reduces or prevents other components of negative well-being including anxiety, hopelessness, and behavioral problems, and is effective for children of different cultural and racial backgrounds (Seligman et al. 2009).

The program's impact on the more positive components of children's lives has recently been assessed (Gillham and Bernard 2011). Both academic grades and social skills increase for children participating in some form of this "Virtue in

M. D. Holder, *Happiness in Children*, SpringerBriefs in Well-Being and Quality of Life Research, DOI: 10.1007/978-94-007-4414-1_9, © The Author(s) 2012

Action" program, as described above. These improvements occurred for children with average academic achievement, but not for honors students. However, the program did not produce an increase in measures of positive subjective well-being, including happiness. Nonetheless, given that 20–24% of children and adolescents experience a major depressive episode by age 18 (Lewinsohn et al. 1998), the Penn Resiliency Program is important if it can help prevent and reduce depressive symptoms in pre-adults.

Hope: Another approach to promoting well-being in children involves hope-based interventions. These interventions are closely associated with positive psychology. However, unlike the Penn Resiliency Program, the hope-based interventions are typically designed to increase hope and are assessed in terms of their ability to promote positive subjective well-being.

Relative to several other dimensions of well-being, hope has been more thoroughly researched in children. Hope can be conceptualized as a human strength reflected in conceptualizing clear goals, developing specific strategies to achieve these goals, and having the motivation to initiate and maintain these strategies (Snyder 1994, 2002). Part of the reason that the study of hope in children is more mature than other constructs related to well-being is attributable to the development of a scale specifically designed to assess hope in 7 to 14 year-old children: the Children's Hope Scale (Snyder et al. 1997). Research has shown that hope is positively correlated with global life satisfaction in middle-school students (Marques et al. 2007), and negatively correlated with symptoms of depression in children (Snyder et al. 1997). Furthermore, hope in children is positively associated with a wide range of positive attributes including optimism, mental health, academic achievement, and superior athletic performance (Lopez et al. 2008).

Research has shown that interventions focusing on promoting the hope of children in schools are beneficial (Lopez et al. 2008). As previously described, a 5-week intervention was completed for 10–12-year-old children in a school setting (Marques et al. 2011). Children who experienced the intervention showed increased levels of life satisfaction, hope, and self-worth, which were maintained when assessed during an 18-month follow-up. Studies that assess the efficacy of hope-based exercises show that psychological strengths in children can be promoted with relatively short interventions. The research on hope suggests a template to develop and assess programs designed to enhance children's positive well-being. These programs may have a realistic possibility of being adopted given their relatively short duration.

References

Brunwasser, S. M., Gillham, J. E., & Kim, E. S. (2009). A meta-analytic review of the penn resiliency program's effect on depressive symptoms. *Journal of Consulting and Clinical Psychology, 77*, 1042–1054.

Gillham, J. & Bernard, M. (2011). Teaching positive psychology to adolescents: 3 year follow-up. Second World Congress on Positive Psychology, Philadelphia.

Lewinsohn, P. M., Rohde, P., & Seeley, J. R. (1998). Major depressive disorder in older adolescents: Prevalance, risk factors, and clinical implications. *Clinical Psychology Review, 18*, 765–794.

Lopez, S. J., Rose, S., Robinson, C., Marques, S. C., & Pais-Ribeiro, J. (2008). Measuring and promoting hope in school children. In R. Gilman, E. S. Huebner, & M. J. Furlong (Eds.), *Handbook of positive psychology in the schools* (pp. 37–51). Mahwah: Lawrence Erlbaum.

Marques, S. C., Pais-Ribeiro, J. L., & Lopez, S. J. (2007). *Hope in relation to life satisfaction, mental health, and self-worth in students.* Poster presented at the Xth European Congress of Psychology. Prague, Czech Republic.

Marques, S. C., Lopez, S. J., & Pais-Ribeiro, J. L. (2011). Building hope for the future: strengths in middle-school students. *Journal of Happiness Studies, 12*, 139–152.

Seligman, M., Ernst, R., Gillham, J., Reivich, K., & Linkins, M. (2009). Positive education: positive psychology and classroom interventions. *Oxford Review of Education, 35*, 293–311.

Snyder, C. R. (1994). *The psychology of hope: you can get there from here.* New York: Free Press.

Snyder, C. R., Hoza, B., Pelham, W. E., Raphoff, M., Ware, L., Danovsky, M., et al. (1997). The development and validation of the children's hope scale. *Journal of Pediatric Psychology, 22*, 399–421.

Snyder, C. R. (2002). Hope theory: rainbows in the mind. *Psychological Inquiry, 13*, 249–275.

Chapter 10
Future Research

Effective measures of children's well-being have been developed through empirical research. Using these measures, studies have identified many of the correlates and predictors of children's well-being including their happiness, as well as assisted in developing and testing interventions to enhance children's well-being. Researchers can now use these findings to help formulate future research questions and guide their development of research designs. Given that research has established relationships between temperament and well-being, future descriptive studies could incorporate measures of temperament. For example, this would allow studies to determine how much a variable of interest contributes to children's happiness over and above the contribution of temperament, in much the same way as research on adults' happiness incorporates measures of personality (Holder and Coleman 2008; Holder and Klassen 2010). Ciarrocchi Dy-Liacco and Deneke (2008) used this approach to find that aspects of religiousness and spirituality were significant predictors of hope and optimism in adults over and above the variance accounted for by the five-factor model of personality. Similarly, Lu and Hu (2005) conducted a study of Chinese university students and found that satisfaction with leisure experiences was a significant predictor of happiness even after extraversion and neuroticism were accounted for.

Using a parallel approach, studies of children's well-being could assess temperament to determine whether the variables of interest contribute to well-being, beyond the contribution of temperament traits. However, studying the relationship between adult personality and subjective well-being at the trait level may be limited. Steel et al. (2008) emphasized that the trait level may be too broad because the individual facets that comprise each trait may not all equally contribute to well-being. Additionally, these facets may not all correlate with well-being in the same direction. Furthermore, some facets of a trait may not be related to well-being at all. As a result, research that only assesses personality at the trait level may give misleading results. For example, research may show that a given trait is not related to well-being; however, individual facets of this trait may still

M. D. Holder, *Happiness in Children*, SpringerBriefs in Well-Being and Quality of Life Research, DOI: 10.1007/978-94-007-4414-1_10, © The Author(s) 2012

have quite strong relationships with well-being. Steel et al. (2008) suggest that the study of the relationship between personality and well-being may be more informative if personality was studied at the facet level. Similarly, studies of the relationship between well-being and temperament in children may benefit from a more detailed perspective by considering the components of each temperament trait rather than the aggregated measure at the trait level.

An additional major focus of positive psychology research with children should be on evaluating the efficacy of interventions designed to enhance children's positive well-being. Research has validated that some interventions can support enduring improvements in well-being (Sheldon and Lyubomirsky 2004). However, very few studies have tested strategies designed to enhance well-being in children (Holder and Callaway 2010). A meta-analysis of 150 experimental, ambulatory, and longitudinal studies of the impact of well-being on objective measures of health suggested that positive well-being has a beneficial impact on health, possibly through bolstering immune functioning (Howell et al. 2007). However, only six of the 150 studies were conducted with pre-adults and most of these six employed adolescents. Similarly, a meta-analysis of 51 studies of positive psychology interventions may provide limited insight into enhancing children's well-being (Sin and Lyubomirsky 2009). This meta-analysis concluded that interventions can promote positive feelings, behaviors and cognitions. The authors concluded that the interventions were most effective for those people who were older, had higher initial levels of depression, were motivated to participate in an intervention, and were provided with an individualized intervention.

The conclusion that interventions are more effective for older people should not be interpreted as showing that children are less likely to benefit from positive psychology interventions. This conclusion may not apply to children because the meta-analysis did not include substantial research on children. Relatively few studies of positive psychology interventions using children exist and, therefore, few were selected for the meta-analysis. The impact of interventions on children and their well-being is not yet determined. For example, interventions in schools have been employed to reduce or prevent bullying. The results of these studies have been mixed with only some showing success (Smith et al. 2004). However, it is possible that even if a program is successful in reducing bullying, the subjective well-being of children may not be enhanced. This possibility should be assessed. In fact, the complement of this possibility has been demonstrated in at least one study. Houlston and Smith (2009) assessed a program designed to address bullying. They used a longitudinal approach with both qualitative and quantitative measures. Though they found that the program did not contribute to a decrease in bullying or victimization, they found positive improvements in the children's perspectives of their schools and an improvement in self-esteem.

Research with adults has determined that some strategies effectively and enduringly increase aspects of well-being (Seligman et al. 2005). For example, counting blessings in one's life can enhance well-being in adults (Emmons and McCullough 2003) and young adolescents (Froh et al. 2008). Moreover, in one of the most rigorous investigations to date of multiple strategies designed to enduringly increase happiness, Seligman et al. (2005) showed that three of five tested interventions increased participants' happiness and decreased depression up to 6 months post-intervention, compared to a placebo-controlled group.

Few studies have tested strategies designed to enhance well-being in children, even though most adults strongly desire children to be happy. Thus, an important next step in the study of well-being in children should include identifying programs that allow children, parents, and educators to promote well-being in children. We should be cautious in adopting a "one size fits all" model of promoting children's well-being. It is quite likely that the efficacy of any intervention interacts with individual differences stemming from temperament, culture, gender, motivation, and age. At a relatively simple level, researchers have designed and tested an intervention based on writing and delivering a letter that expresses gratitude to someone in their life who has made a positive difference but gone relatively unnoticed. This intervention has been employed with children, and the children typically address the letter to one of their parents. However, the efficacy of this task might be reduced for children who have high levels of shyness, because of a possible increase in the anxiety they might experience in a situation of such personal expression.

Individual differences in personality also play a role in the normal day-to-day lives of people choosing ways to enhance their positive well-being. Individual adults pursue different strategies, based in part on their personalities, in an attempt to promote their happiness (Tkach and Lyubomirsky 2006). Thus, it is possible that children select ways to increase their happiness as a function of their temperament. Therefore, those seeking to promote happiness in children should also consider how individual differences in temperament may influence the selection and effectiveness of strategies related to promoting children's well-being.

As examples of possible future avenues for research on children's well-being, the next three sections discuss three potentially fruitful areas of study: (1) the "fit" between the child and positive psychology interventions, using computer gaming as an example, (2) the well-being of children who belong to vulnerable, or at risk, populations, and (3) extending work on the "other praising" emotions to children with an emphasis on elevation.

Fit and Computer Gaming: Even some of the earliest investigations designed to assess the efficacy of strategies to enhance positive subjective well-being recognized that there is no "one size fits all" strategy. For example, Fordyce (1983) taught undergraduate students to emphasize fourteen characteristics found in people with high levels of happiness. These characteristics included spending an increased time socializing, and reducing the amount that they worried. By emulating the attitudes and behaviors of happy people, the students were able to increase their happiness, and some students were able to sustain this increase for at least one year. Some strategies were more effective for some individuals than others. Importantly, Fordyce noted that the "fit" between the person and the strategy was an important determinant in how effective each strategy was. More recent work has reached a similar conclusion. For example, Sheldon and Lyubomirsky (2004), investigated strategies designed to have an enduring increase on positive well-being. Similar to Fordyce, they concluded that individual characteristics are important determinants of an intervention's capacity to enhance well-being. In particular, effectiveness was partially determined by the personality and individual goals of the participants.

The Self-Concordance Model (Sheldon and Houser-Marko 2001) provides a theoretical context for the notion of fit, which can be applied to examining strategies to promote well-being. According to this model, participants' willingness to maintain exercises to attain goals, and the resulting success of these exercises is affected by individual differences. People are more likely to be successful in achieving goals if the goals reflect their internal values and interests. Those who adopt goals, and the strategies to attain them, that reflect external pressures and values are often less successful. In order to increase adherence to programs and exercises to enhance well-being, people, including children, should be mindful of selecting strategies that are in good agreement with their dispositions and preferences.

Given the concept of fit and the Self-Concordance Model, successful strategies to enhance well-being in children should be mindful of children's individual interests. These strategies will be more successful if they are centered on activities that children prefer and participate in without external pressure. Adherence to interventions, with the purpose of enhancing well-being, can be undermined if people increasingly find that the tasks become a chore. By developing strategies around activities that children are internally motivated to engage in, the likelihood that the children will maintain their participation in the program may be increased.

Playing video games is clearly an activity that most children are highly motivated to participate in. An astounding 99% of boys and 94% of girls report playing video games (Lenhart et al. 2008). Adolescents now spend more time playing video games than watching television (Huston et al. 1999) demonstrating that playing computer games is a highly preferred activity for children. Therefore, one possible category of strategies that may be a good fit for children involves those strategies that involve video games. Given that children are intrinsically motivated to play video games, games may afford a valuable opportunity to develop exercises that children will be self-motivated to participate in. Self-determination theory claims that intrinsic motivation and autonomy (e.g., choosing one's own strategies to enhance well-being), in the absence of coercion, are required for human flourishing (Ryan et al. 2006).

However, more video games are centered on violence and aggressions than human flourishing. As a result, researchers have focused on the potentially negative consequences of gaming. These consequences include that playing violent video games may increase aggressive thoughts, behavior, and affect, and decrease prosocial behavior (Anderson 2004; Anderson and Bushman 2001; Funk et al. 2003). For instance, after playing violent video games, people set higher levels of punishment for others and were less likely to help someone in distress (Bartholow and Anderson 2002). Violent games (e.g., Mortal Combat) can increase aggression in males even 24 h after one stops playing, whereas nonviolent games (e.g., Guitar Hero) do not show these effects (Bushman and Gibson 2011).

A recent meta-analysis concluded that playing violent video games increases aggressive behaviors across culture and gender (Anderson et al. 2010), but some studies have not found support for the causal link between playing violent video games and increased aggression (Ferguson et al. 2008; Weigman and van Schie 1998; William and Skoric 2005). Of particular relevance to this point, one meta-analysis failed to find conclusive evidence that a relationship between violent video games and aggression exists (Ferguson and Kilburn 2009). This analysis suggested that those studies that found a relationship between media violence and aggression had several shortcomings. These shortcomings included that they used poor measures of aggression, they did not employ appropriate methodology, and they failed to control for important third variables.

Perhaps the inconsistent results of studies of video game violence and aggression may be found in individual differences. Just as the success of interventions on positive subjective well-being varies between individuals, the influence of gaming on violence and aggression is likely not identical for all people. If specific personality traits predispose individuals to being easily influenced by violent video games, then failing to control for these traits could result in the inconsistencies observed in the literature. Studies have shown that participants high in traits of psychoticism and aggressiveness are more influenced by exposure to violent video games than participants not high in these traits (Arriaga et al. 2006; Markey and Sherer 2009). Additionally, Markey and Markey (2010) performed an archival study and found that individuals high in neuroticism and low on agreeableness and conscientiousness are most influenced by the effects of violent video games.

Theories have been used to help understand how gaming can affect behavior. One theory used to explain the mechanism by which media, including playing video games, can influence thoughts and behaviors is the General Learning Model (GLM; Buckley and Anderson 2006). The GLM suggests that media exposure influences internal states, which change behavior. The GLM is grounded in social learning theory, suggesting that people are more likely to imitate behaviors if they witness positive consequences following these behaviors. This also means people are less likely to imitate behaviors if they are followed by punishment (Bandura 1965). Therefore, if prosocial behaviors in a video game are rewarded, then players of these games may be more likely to perform similar prosocial acts in the real world. If the GLM applies to video games, then video games provide an excellent opportunity to implement controlled conditions in order to influence thoughts, feelings, and behaviors in a positive way (Gentile et al. 2009). To potentially maximize these benefits for children, popular and respected characters and people could be incorporated into the games. These individuals might perform prosocial behaviors that lead to positive consequences.

Research has shown that observing the actions and appearance of one's avatar influences behaviors and attitudes. An "avatar" in gaming is a computer character that represents the player in the game. In a sense, an avatar is one's alter ego in the video game. Players who were given taller avatars behaved more aggressively in online negotiations than players given shorter avatars (Yee et al. 2009). Further, when interacting face-to-face with an experimenter after playing the game, players who had been given taller avatars negotiated more aggressively than those who had been given shorter avatars. The effects of exposure to avatars have the potential to be quite negative. For example, when undergraduates were exposed to a female avatar with a highly sexualized appearance (i.e., suggestively dressed and a responsive high eye gaze) they later exhibited more negative attitudes toward women (Fox and Bailenson 2009b). However, the influence of avatars has the potential to be quite positive. For instance, when undergraduates were exposed to an avatar that represented themselves, they were more likely to copy its actions. Viewing an avatar running on a treadmill increased the likelihood of undergraduates following suit, compared to if the avatar was simply loitering, or if the avatar exercised but did not resemble the viewer (Fox and Bailenson 2009a). This positive effect of increased exercise was observed in a follow-up assessment 24 h after viewing the avatar running.

If violent and aggressive video games influence people in negative ways, prosocial video games might influence people in positive ways. Based on their meta-analysis, Anderson et al. (2010) concluded that exposure to violent video games promotes aggressive behavior in a wide range of people, and they acknowledged the unfortunate lack of research on the positive effects of video games.

Only a few studies have assessed the positive effects of video games. Gentile et al. (2009) found that after playing a prosocial video game, undergraduates engaged in more prosocial behaviors. Similarly, Greitemeyer and Osswald (2010) found that after participants played prosocial video games for 8–10 min, they were much more likely to engage in several prosocial behaviors: helping a harassed experimenter, helping the experimenter pick up spilled pencils, and volunteering for future experiments. Though many of the studies investigate the effects of gaming on adults and adolescents, the positive effects of playing prosocial video games may extend to children. Singaporean children showed a positive relationship between the amount of time they spent playing prosocial video games, and overall prosocial traits and behaviors (Chen et al. 2009). Although this finding does not demonstrate cause and effect, it supports the relationship between prosocial gaming and prosocial behavior in children as a research topic in need of further exploration.

In addition to influencing behavior, prosocial video game play can increase prosocial thoughts (Greitemeyer and Osswald 2009). In one study, participants played a prosocial video game called Lemmings for 10 min. The object of this game was to save the lives of lemmings by herding them toward a safe exit. Compared to individuals who played the neutral puzzle game Tetris for 10 min, those who played Lemmings displayed decreased antisocial affect, increased prosocial affect, and enhanced interpersonal empathy (Greitemeyer et al. 2010). An increase in prosocial thoughts is likely the basis of the increase in prosocial behaviors observed in similar studies (Gentile et al. 2009; Greitemeyer and Osswald 2010).

Conversely, some theories and studies do not support the proposition that playing prosocial video games will increase positive well-being in children. Playing many types of video games can be characterized as an individual activity and activities that promote individual goals may decrease well-being, whereas activities that promote social affiliation and community involvement increase well-being. Nonetheless, empirical studies demonstrate that interacting with an avatar can increase dimensions related to real social interactions.

Though the focus here is on children, the popularity of video games is not restricted to youth; the average age of "video gamers" is 37 years old (Entertainment Software Association 2012). Therefore, developing games designed to enhance well-being may be a good fit for adults as well as children.

Mindfulness and Yoga in Children: Mindfulness refers to the elevated awareness of, and attention to, one's present reality and current experience (Brown and Ryan 2003). Practicing mindfulness has been associated with increases in psychological well-being in adults (Brown and Ryan 2003). Overall, people who practice mindfulness, either in their daily routines or in experientially assigned conditions, realize several benefits including improvements in mental well-being, physical health, behavioral regulation, and interpersonal interactions (Brown et al. 2007). Research on developing and assessing strategies that employ mindfulness as a means to enhance well-being is in a relatively early stage. A main focus of this research has been to use mindfulness as a type of clinical intervention (Branstrom et al. 2010; Fledderus et al. 2010; Lee and Bang 2010).

Though the benefits associated with mindfulness are related to domains associated with well-being in youth and children, research on the efficacy of mindfulness to promote and maintain well-being in these age groups is quite limited. A review by Burke (2010) concluded that there are relatively few studies assessing mindfulness-based interventions with children and youth. Burke was only able to discuss a total of 15 studies with this focus because additional studies do not exist. Furthermore, several of these studies primarily assessed the efficacy of mindfulness-based interventions to alleviate aspects of negative subjective well-being (i.e., anxiety, depression, non-compliance, aggression, and substance use), rather than efficacy to promote positive well-being (i.e., happiness, life satisfaction, social skills, self-control, self-efficacy; Burke 2010).

Given that there are a limited number of studies that investigate the effectiveness of mindfulness-based practices in promoting positive well-being in children, and that these practices are effective with adults, this suggests a potentially fruitful direction of future research. Specifically, this future research would benefit from the development of a mindfulness scale that is valid and sensitive when used with children. This scale could then be used to develop and assess the efficacy of mindfulness training programs in schools, at home, and during extracurricular activities. In turn, the impact of these programs on the promotion and maintenance of children's happiness and life satisfaction could then be assessed using appropriate measures of well-being.

Similar to the practice of mindfulness, the practice of yoga has been associated with improvements in well-being in both clinical and nonclinical adults

(Sharma et al. 2008). Some of the benefits of practicing yoga include a reduction in symptoms associated with depression and chronic disease, and an increase in immune functioning, mindfulness, and attention to daily life (Salmon et al. 2009 and Raub 2002).

Yoga was developed in part to achieve three desired states: (1) development of a strong, flexible, and pain free body, (2) development of a healthy nervous system in which all physiological systems operate at an optimal level, and (3) development of a calm, clear, and peaceful mind (Kayley-Isley et al. 2010). Children and youth may experience positive outcomes from training and practicing yoga in the form of a wide range of benefits (Kayley-Isley et al. 2010). These benefits might include improvements in negative well-being (e.g., decreased anxiety, decreased depression, decreased breathing problems associated with asthma, and weight loss) as well as positive well-being (e.g., improved self-concept, body satisfaction, attention, and overall well-being).

Empirical research has supported the position that practicing yoga benefits school-aged children. Positive results were observed in a recent study of children who participated in a yoga training program at school (Case-Smith et al. 2010). Children who participated in the program felt calmer and more focused as suggested by interviews and art-based techniques. These children also generated more ideas for controlling their behavior in stressful situations and found improvements to their self-esteem. Although research has begun to provide evidence that yoga provides benefits to children in terms of reducing negative well-being and promoting aspects of positive well-being, one avenue of future research would be to assess the impact of practicing yoga on children's happiness and life satisfaction.

Assessing and Enhancing Happiness in Vulnerable Populations: The research literature on children's positive subjective well-being, including happiness, is limited, and research on assessing and promoting well-being in vulnerable populations of children is almost completely absent.

There is a sparse but developing literature on the well-being of vulnerable adults. For example, the happiness of people with physical disabilities was compared to people without physical disabilities (Marinić and Brkljačić 2008). On average, using a 10-point happiness scale, those with disabilities scored 1.5 points below those without disabilities. In general those with a physical disability still rated themselves above the scale's median which reflected a neutral level of happiness. This study is limited regarding the insights it provides on happiness in children with physical disabilities. Out of the 397 persons with disabilities studied, only seven were less than 20 years old and the majority of the participants acquired their disability during adulthood.

Like studies of physical disabilities, studies of positive well-being in people with cognitive disabilities are primarily restricted to adults. A cross-cultural study of the elderly reported that happiness was lower for people with cognitive impairments (Cooper et al. 2011). The lower levels of happiness were attributed to decreased social networks. Reduced happiness was not an inevitable consequence of dementia, but rather occurred when the levels of social interactions were reduced. When social interactions, including support previously provided by family members, transitioned to being provided by independent sources there was a significant decrease in happiness.

A literature review was particularly interesting as it focused on the expression and assessment of emotions in people with severe or profound intellectual disabilities (Adams and Oliver 2011). Those with dementia and those with schizophrenia were also included in the review. The authors note that for those people with disabilities who have a limited capacity to communicate, no comprehensive or standardized instruments to assess emotions were available. Individuals with schizophrenia express fewer and less intense emotions in general, but may also experience emotions at a similar, or even higher level, than those who were not diagnosed with schizophrenia (Herbener et al. 2008). This may be true of other populations ranging from those in the final stages of dementia to children with autism. However, there are very few studies examining well-being in children with disabilities. For instance, in the 18 studies that Adams and Oliver (2011) focus on, only one (Collis et al. 2008) investigated well-being in children.

Nonetheless, positive psychology may have much to offer vulnerable populations of children. One direction for future research is to identify the common and unique factors that predict positive well-being in vulnerable populations. This will then allow interventions that utilize this information to be developed and tested. An additional direction might be to focus on the caregivers of these children. One research program provided mindfulness training to mothers and reported that their happiness increased and also that their children's behavior improved, including those children with developmental disorders (Singh et al. 2007; Singh et al. 2010).

Elevation: Another potentially fruitful avenue of research with children is the study of "other-praising" emotions, such as elevation, gratitude, and admiration. These emotions may arise from witnessing other people behave in morally exemplary ways. For example, one may experience a warm or glowing feeling after watching a saintly person help others, a politician deliver a moving speech, or being surprised by an ordinary person acting with extraordinary kindness and compassion.

One type of "other-praising" emotion is elevation, which is characterized by a warm uplifting feeling following the observation of people behaving in ways that demonstrate moral beauty or virtue (Haidt 2000). Elevation can act as a catalyst to motivate the observer to connect with others and to engage in prosocial behaviors. Though the feelings associated with other-praising emotions are linked to positive affect, they can be distinguished from those positive emotions (joy and amusement) which have received more research attention (Algoe and Haidt 2009).

Research has not focused on other-praising emotions in children, but these emotions may provide an important and promising research area. Children are experts at observing others and learning from these observations. Additionally, research in psychology has studied the resilience of children as they maintain functioning, even when faced with horrific challenges. More recent research has focused on post-traumatic growth, in which some children respond to major challenges by achieving a higher, more successful, and productive level of functioning than before the challenge. However, for both resiliency and post-traumatic growth, the critical stimulus is a terrible event. Perhaps in addition to the study of responses to negative trauma, we need to study children who experience inspiring events; we could call this a post-ecstatic growth. Both trauma and inspiring events share certain features. Together, they create a sense of awe related to the vastness of the experience, and require some form of accommodation on the part of the person experiencing them. A study of post-ecstatic growth would need to include research that is focused on the gains children experience in the absence of pain and suffering.

References

Adams, D., & Oliver, C. (2011). The expression and assessment of emotions and internal states in individuals with severe or profound intellectual disabilities. *Clinical Psychology Review, 31*, 293–306.

Algoe, S. B., & Haidt, J. (2009). Witnessing excellence in action: The *other-praising* emotions of elevation, gratitude, and admiration. *The Journal of Positive Psychology, 4*, 105–127.

Anderson, C. A. (2004). An update on the effects of violent video games. *Journal of Adolescence, 27*, 113–122.

Anderson, C. A., & Bushman, B. J. (2001). Effects of violent video games on aggressive behavior, aggressive cognition, aggressive affect, physiological arousal, and prosocial behavior: A meta-analytic review of the scientific literature. *Psychological Science, 12*, 353–359.

Anderson, C. A., Shibuya, A., Ihori, N., Swing, E. L., Bushman, B. J., Sakamoto, A., et al. (2010). Violent video game effects on aggression, empathy, and prosocial behavior in eastern and western countries: A meta-analytic review. *Psychological Bulletin, 136*, 151–173.

Arriaga, P., Esteves, F., Carneiro, P., & Monteiro, M. B. (2006). Violent computer games and their effects on state hostility and physiological arousal. *Aggressive Behavior, 32*, 358–371.

Bandura, A. (1965). Influence of models' reinforecement contingencies on the acquisition of imitative responses. *Journal of Personality and Social Psychology, 1*, 589–595.

Bartholow, B. D., & Anderson, C. A. (2002). Effects of violent video games on aggressive behavior. *Journal of Experimental Social Psychology, 38*, 283–290.

Branstrom, R., Kvillemo, P., Brandberg, Y., & Moskowitz, J. T. (2010). Self-report mindfulness as a mediator of psychological well-being in a stress-reduction intervention for cancer patients- A randomized study. *Annals of Behavioural Medicine, 39*, 151–161.

Brown, K. W., & Ryan, R. M. (2003). The benefits of being present: Mindfulness and its role in psychological well-being. *Journal o Personality and Social Psychology, 84*, 822–848.

Brown, K. W., Ryan, R. M., & Creswell, J. D. (2007). Mindfulness: Theoretical foundations and evidence for its salutary effects. *Psychological Inquiry, 18*, 211–237.

Buckley, K. E., & Anderson, C. A. (2006). A theoretical model of the effects and consequences of playing video games. In P. Vorderer & J. Bryant (Eds.), *Playing video games: Motives, responses, and consequences* (pp. 363–378). Mahwah: Erlbaum.

Burke, C. A. (2010). Mindfulness-based approaches with children and adolescents: A preliminary review of current research in an emergent field. *Journal of Child and Family Studies, 19*, 133–144.

Bushman, B. J., & Gibson, B. (2011). Violent video games cause an increase in aggression long after the game has been turned off. *Social Psychological and Personality Science, 2*, 29–32.

Case-Smith, J., Sines, J. S., & Klatt, M. (2010). Perceptions of children who participated in a school-based yoga program. *Journal of Occupational Therapy, Schools, and Early Intervention, 3*, 226–238.

Chen, V. H., Lin, W., Ng, C. W., Chai, S. L., Khoo, A. C. E., & Duh, H. B. (2009). Children's choice of games: The influence of prosocial tendency and education-Level. *Entertainment Computing, 5709*, 110–119.

Ciarrocchi, J. W., Dy-Liacco, G. S., & Deneke, E. (2008). Gods or rituals? Relational faith, spiritual discontent, and religious practices as predictors of hope and optimism. *The Journal of Positive Psychology, 3*, 120–136.

Collis, L., Moss, J., Jutley, J., Cornish, K., & Oliver, C. (2008). Facial expressions of affect in children with Cornelia de Lange syndrome. *Journal of Intellectual Disability Research, 52*, 207–215.

Cooper, C., Bebbington, P., & Livingston, G. (2011). Cognitive impairment and happiness in older people in low and middle income countries: Results from the 10/66 study. *Journal of Affective Disorders, 130*, 198–204.

Emmons, R. A., & McCullough, M. E. (2003). Counting blessings versus burdens: An experimental investigation of gratitude and subjective well-being in daily life. *Journal of Personality and Social Psychology, 84*, 377–389.

Entertainment Software Association (2012). Industry facts. http://www.theesa.com/facts/index.asp

Ferguson, C. J., & Kilburn, J. (2009). The public health risks of media violence: A meta-analytic review. *Journal of Pediatrics, 154*, 759–763.

Ferguson, C. J., Rueda, S. M., Cruz, A. M., Ferguson, D. E., Fritz, S., & Smith, S. M. (2008). Violent video games and aggression: Causal relationship or byproduct of family violence and intrinsic violence motivation? *Criminal Justice and Behavior, 35*, 311–332.

Fledderus, M., Bohlmeijer, E. T., Smit, F., & Westerhof, G. J. (2010). Mental health promotion as a new goal in public mental health care: A randomized controlled trial of an intervention enhancing psychological flexibility. *American Journal of Public Health, 100*, 2372–2378.

Fordyce, M. W. (1983). A program to increase happiness: Further studies. *Journal of Counselling Psychology, 30*, 483–498.

Fox, J., & Bailenson, J. N. (2009a). Virtual virgins and vamps: The effects of exposure to female characters' sexualized appearance and gaze in an immersive virtual environment. *Sex Roles, 61*, 147–157.

Fox, J., & Bailenson, J. N. (2009b). Virtual self-modeling: The effects of vicarious reinforcement and identification on exercise behaviors. *Media Psychology, 12*, 1–25.

Froh, J. J., Sefick, W. J., & Emmons, R. A. (2008). Counting blessings in early adolescents: An experimental study of gratitude and subjective well-being. *Journal of School Psychology, 46*, 213–233.

Funk, J. B., Buchman, D. D., Jenks, J., & Bechtoldt, H. (2003). Playing violent video games, desensitization, and moral evaluation in children. *Journal of Applied Developmental Psychology, 24*, 413–436.

Gentile, D. A., Anderson, C. A., Yukawa, S., Ihori, N., Saleem, M., Ming, L. K., et al. (2009). The effects of prosocial video games on prosocial behaviors: International evidence from correlational, longitudinal and experimental studies. *Personality and Social Psychology Bulletin, 25*, 752–763.

Greitemeyer, T., & Osswald, S. (2009). Prosocial video games reduce aggressive cognitions. *Journal of Experimental Social Psychology, 45*, 896–900.

Greitemeyer, T., & Osswald, S. (2010). Effects of prosocial video games on prosocial behavior. *Journal of Personality and Social Psychology, 98*, 211–221.

Greitemeyer, T., Osswald, S., & Brauer, M. (2010). Playing prosocial video games increases empathy and decreases shadenfreude. *Emotion, 10*, 796–802.

Haidt, J. (2000). The positive emotion of elevation. *Prevention and Treatment, 3*, 1–5.

Herbener, E. S., Song, W., Khine, T. T., & Sweeney, J. A. (2008). What aspects of emotional functioning are impaired in schizophrenia? *Schizophrenia Research, 98*, 239–246.

Holder, M. D., & Coleman, B. (2008). The contribution of temperament, popularity, and physical appearance to children's happiness. *Journal of Happiness Studies, 9*, 279–302.

Holder, M. D., & Callaway, R. (2010). Happiness in children: A review of the scientific literature. In F. Columbus (Ed.), *The Psychology of Happiness*, (pp. 51–70). Nova Science Publishers Inc:.

Holder, M. D., & Klassen, A. (2010). Temperament and happiness in children. *Journal of Happiness Studies, 11*, 419–439.

Houlston, C., & Smith, P. K. (2009). The impact of a peer counseling scheme to address bullying in an all-girl London school: A longitudinal study. *British Journal of Educational Psychology, 79*, 69–86.

Howell, R. T., Kern, M. L., & Lyubomirsky, S. (2007). Health benefits: Meta-analytically determining the impact of well-being on objective health outcomes. *Health Psychology Review, 1*, 83–136.

Huston, A. C., Wright, J. C., Marquis, J., & Green, S. B. (1999). How young children spend their time: Television and other activities. *Developmental Psychology, 35*, 912–925.

Kayley-Isley, L. C., Peterson, J., Fischer, C., & Peterson, E. (2010). Yoga as a complimentary therapy for children and adolescents: A guide for clinicians. *Psychiatry, 7*, 20–32.

Lee, W. K., & Bang, H. J. (2010). The effects of mindfulness-based group intervention on the mental health of middle-aged Korean women in community. *Stress and Health, 26*, 341–348.

Lenhart, A., Kahne, J., Middaugh, E., Macgill, E. R., Evans, C., & Vitak, J. (2008, September 16). Teens, video games, and civics. Washington, DC: Pew Internet; American Life Project.

Lu, L., & Hu, C. (2005). Personality, leisure experiences and happiness. *Journal of Happiness Studies, 6*, 325–342.

Marinić, M., & Brkljačić, T. (2008). Love over gold—the correlations of happiness level with some life satisfaction factors between persons with and without physical disability. *Journal of Developmental Physical Disabilities, 20*, 527–540.

Markey, P. M., & Markey, C. N. (2010). Vulnerability to violent video games: A review and integration of personality research. *Review of General Psychology, 12*, 82–91.

Markey, P. M., & Scherer, K. (2009). An examination of psychoticism and motion capture controls as moderators of the effects of violent video games. *Computers in Human Behavior, 25*, 407–411.

Raub, J. A. (2002). Psychophysiologic effects of hatha yoga on musculoskeletal and cardiopulmonary function: A literature review. *The Journal of Alternative and Complementary Medicine, 8*, 797–812.

Ryan, R. M., Huta, V., & Deci, E. L. (2006). Living well: A self-determining theory perspective on eudaimonia. *Journal of Happiness Studies, 9*, 139–170.

Salmon, P., Lush, E., Jablonski, M., & Sephton, S. E. (2009). Yoga and mindfulness: Clinical aspects of an ancient mind/body practice. *Cognitive and Behavioural Practice, 16*, 59–72.

Seligman, M. E. P., Steen, T. A., & Park, N. (2005). Positive psychology progress: Empirical validation of interventions. *American Psychologist, 60*, 410–421.

Sharma, R., Gupta, N., & Bijlani, R. L. (2008). Effect of yoga based lifestyle intervention on subjective well being. *Indian Journal of Physiological Pharmacology, 52*, 123–131.

Sheldon, K. M., & Houser-Marko, L. (2001). Self-concordance, goal attainment, and the pursuit of happiness: Can there be an upward spiral? *Journal of Personality and Social Psychology, 80*, 152–165.

Sheldon, K. M., & Lyubomirsky, S. (2004). Achieving sustainable new happiness: Prospects, practices, and prescriptions. In A. Linley & S. Joseph (Eds.), *Positive psychology in practice* (pp. 127–145). Hoboken: Wiley.

Sin, N. L., & Lyubomirsky, S. (2009). *Enhancing well-being and alleviating depressive symptoms with positive psychology interventions: A practice-friendly meta-analysis. Journal of Clinical Psychology: In Session, 65*, 467–487.

Singh, N. N., Lancioni, G. E., Winton, A. S. W., Singh, J., Curtis, J. W., Wahler, R. G., et al. (2007). Mindful parenting decreases aggression and increases social behavior in children with profound developmental disabilities. *Behavior Modification, 31*, 749–771.

Singh, N. N., Lancioni, G. E., Winton, A. S. W., Singh, J., Adkins, A. D., & Wahler, R. G. (2010). Training in mindful caregiving transfers to parent-child interactions. *Journal of Child and Family Studies, 19*, 167–174.

Smith, P. K., Pepler, D., & Rigby, K. (2004). *Bullying in schools: How successful can interventions be?*. New York: Cambridge University Press.

Steel, P., Schmidt, J., & Shultz, J. (2008). Refining the relationship between personality and subjective well-being. *Psychological Bulletin, 134*, 138–161.

Tkach, C., & Lyubomirsky, S. (2006). How do people pursue happiness?: Relating personality, happiness-increasing strategies and well-being. *Journal of Happiness Studies, 7*, 183–225.

Weigman, O., & van Schie, E. (1998). Video game playing and its relations with aggressive and prosocial behavior. *British Journal of Social Psychology, 37*, 367–378.

William, D., & Skoric, M. (2005). Internet fantasy violence: A test of aggression in an online game. *Communication Monographs, 72*, 217–233.

Yee, N., Bailenson, J. N., & Ducheneaut, N. (2009). The proteus effect: Implications of transformed digital self-representation on online and offline behavior. *Communication Research, 36*, 285–312.

Chapter 11
Conclusion

There is now a substantial literature on positive subjective well-being. Though researchers in psychology and medicine have traditionally focused on identifying and alleviating illness, pain, discomfort, and negative affect, more recently positive psychologists have emphasized promoting factors that contribute to human flourishing. This emphasis has not yet placed significant attention on children. It is particularly important to develop comprehensive, standardized, reliable, and valid methods to assess positive well-being in children. Without these measures, we may be able to determine whether well-intended programs (e.g., anti bullying campaigns) achieve at least some of the desired outcome (e.g., significant reductions in bullying) but we will not be able to ascertain the impact of these programs on a very meaningful level (i.e., determine whether the program enhanced children's well-being). There is a global consensus that we value and desire happiness for our children (Diener and Lucas 2004). Some of the most exciting and valuable current and future contributions of positive psychology include developing an evidence-based understanding of how to support and promote children's flourishing thus enabling them to reach their full potential. By developing and using effective measure of children well-being, we can focus on and assess the efficacy of strategies to promote children's positive well-being.

Reference

Diener, M. L., & Lucas, R. E. (2004). Adults' desires for children's emotions across 48 countries: Association with individual and national characteristics. *Journal of Cross-Cultural Psychology, 35*, 525–547.

M. D. Holder, *Happiness in Children*, SpringerBriefs in Well-Being and Quality of Life Research, DOI: 10.1007/978-94-007-4414-1_11, © The Author(s) 2012